HOLLYWOOD

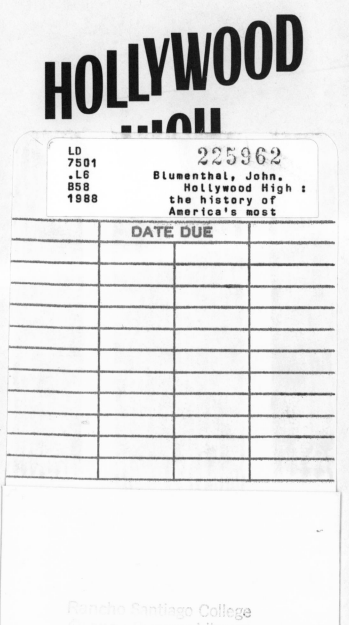

DATE DUE

Other Books by John Blumenthal

The Case of the Hardboiled Dicks

Love's Reckless Rash (coauthor)

The Official Hollywood Handbook

The Tinseltown Murders

WOOD

THE HISTORY OF AMERICA'S · MOST FAMOUS PUBLIC SCHOOL

HOLLYWOOD HIGH SCHOOL · ACHIEVE THE HONORABLE

JOHN BLUMENTHAL

BALLANTINE BOOKS · NEW YORK

CONTENTS

ACKNOWLEDGMENTS

This book would have been close to impossible to research and write without the kindness and assistance of a number of individuals. I am especially grateful to Hollywood High's former principal, Willard B. Hansen, who gave generously of his time and energy for the duration of this project. School librarian Beverly Taylor was also very helpful in expediting my search for materials.

In addition, I would like to extend my sincere thanks to those faculty members and alumni of Hollywood High who were kind enough to share their reminiscences with me. Among them: Alexis Smith, Fay Wray, Joel McCrea, Mike Farrell, Warren Christopher, John Ritter, Barbara Hershey, Robert Carradine, Bill Lindsay, Glenn McConnell, Phyllis Zimmerman, Lillian Copple, Cyrille Garfield, Chester Taft, Ruth Sherwood, Lois Weber, Jerry Melton, John Ingle, Sylvia Sims, and many, many others.

Thanks also to Lynn Seligman, Joe Blades, Bob Wyatt, Ingrid van Eckert, Pat Jennings, and Sue Russell for their help, guidance, and encouragement

Hollywood High. Bigger 'n life. The most famous high school in the whole wide world. And all I had to do was get up in the morning and walk to it.

—Carol Burnett

We rattled our way into Los Angeles—the biggest city I'd ever seen, its wide streets lined with ornate stone buildings, with bright, imposing signs. And I was really impressed with the new building on the corner where we waited, with a façade as broad and white as a movie screen. It was Hollywood High, my new school.

—Lana Turner

HOLLYWOOD HIGH

INTRODUCTION

It is the rare American public high school that cannot boast at least two or three graduates who went on to achieve distinction in one field or another. Some, particularly the old institutions, may even have half a dozen or more. New Trier High School in Illinois, for example, has an impressive list of celebrated alumni, as does Los Angeles's Fairfax High. But no public high school can come close to Hollywood High's record. For sheer numbers alone, the list of its illustrious graduates is close to astounding. Hollywood High, unique among public high schools, is a true phenomenon.

The reasons behind Hollywood High's claim to fame can be summed up in two words: timing and location. The school was simply at the right place at the right time. It was built on the corner of Sunset Boulevard and Highland Avenue in 1905, just six years before the movies came to town. When the filmmakers set up shop in the area, they found it necessary to recruit local talent, and Hollywood High's eager student thespians jumped at the opportunity. After all, what youngster could resist the glitz and glamour that characterized film work from the very beginning, especially when the studios were no more than a hop, skip, and jump from campus?

For more than eighty years, Hollywood High supplied the entertainment industry with everything from ingenues to stunt drivers—and a place to park its child stars between film commitments. Talent scouts regularly sat in on school productions, debates, and speech contests, hoping to make a discovery, and very often they did. In 1936 the school's fame grew immeasurably after one of its students—a ravishing sophomore named Judy Turner—cut a typing class and ran across the street for a soda. Publicists were quick to turn Lana Turner's "discovery" into legend, and Hollywood High was suddenly dubbed "The Star Hatchery." The nickname stuck. That year—1936—Lana Turner, Mickey Rooney, Judy Garland, Nanette Fabray, Marge Champion, and Alexis Smith were all on campus at the same time. In years to come, the school's "Alumni News" column often read like a page out of *Variety*.

Today, visitors to Hollywood High are routinely handed a photocopied list of the school's celebrity graduates. It runs a full two pages, single-spaced, and includes, in addition to those names already mentioned, Fay Wray, Joel McCrea, Sally Kellerman, Jason Robards, Rick Nelson, John Ritter, James Garner, Carol Burnett, Stefanie Powers, and Linda Evans, to cite just a few. (Marilyn Monroe is also on the list, but she doesn't belong there. Marilyn attended a number of local high schools, but Hollywood High was not one of them.)

If the movies had settled in Dubuque, Hollywood High would still have had an estimable celebrity roster.

Nobel prizewinning physicist William Shockley went there, as did journalist Adela Rogers St. John, pianists Gerald Robbins and Horacio Gutierez, Bishop James A. Pike, and the Carter administration's assistant secretary of state, Warren Christopher. But this is hardly surprising when one considers the school's longevity and the fact that, over the years, it has yielded well over sixty thousand alumni.

Naturally, it was Hollywood High's amazing output of celebrity graduates that inspired this history, and much of what follows is devoted to chronicling their high school careers—and revealing who among them were the class clowns, the scholars, the loners, the jocks, the rebels, the delinquents, the geeks. For the most part, the celebrities I interviewed were able to reminisce about their high school years with a remarkable degree of objectivity. After all, who among us does not look back upon those formative years with an odd mixture of nostalgia and embarrassment? It is a time in which we are tragically insecure and uncertain about ourselves, given to vanity and self-consciousness, desperately idealistic and naive; it is a sort of purgatory between childhood and adulthood. In many of those respects, teenagers have not changed all that much in the last eighty years.

Apart from its celebrity alums, the school's history is of interest on another level. Having been established not long after the turn of the century, Hollywood High provides us with not only a record of American teenage life throughout the century, but the rare opportunity to observe the last eighty years of our history through the somewhat peculiar viewpoint of the American teenager. History is usually analyzed and cataloged by adults, and thus it is the adult version of events, values, fashions, and customs that is invariably handed down to us. The American teenager, exiled to the insular world of the high school campus, shielded by protective parents and molded by an upstanding faculty, offers us a purer, fresher, more innocent interpretation. If nothing else, it is an interpretation rife with unintentional humor.

Much of this humor drives from the pages of the student newspaper. Fortunately some farsighted soul had the wisdom to preserve every issue of *The Hollywood High School News* from the year 1918 to the present day. Like that of most school papers, its editorial content was strictly overseen by faculty advisers, and its editors and reporters appear to have been selected more on the basis of right-mindedness than writing skill. In fact, it is not until the advent of the turbulent Sixties that the paper offers us anything resembling independent thinking or dissent. Nevertheless, its voice, though often prim and righteous, provides us with an accurate chronicle of the high jinks of seven decades of American youth. It is from these pages, as well as those of the school yearbooks (dating back to 1906), that I have derived much of this history.

PART ONE

THE EARLY YEARS

1903-1919

1.

A ridiculous piece of extravagance.
—Local farmers' reaction to
spending sixty-seven thousand
dollars on a school building

Once upon a time, in the year 1900 to be exact, Hollywood, California, was little more than an ordinary American farming town. Nobody was taking a meeting; nobody was doing lunch at the Brown Derby; and if anybody was pitching anything, it was most likely hay. True, the town boasted an agreeable climate and was only an hour's carriage drive from the beach, but beyond that Hollywood was nothing to write home about. Most of its five hundred residents—many of them retired people—had settled there to escape the flash and hustle of eastern cities. By most accounts, the Hollywood that existed at the turn of the century was a sleepy, sun-drenched suburb of simple houses and wide open spaces. Mostly wide open spaces.

In those days, before freeways, gridlock, and smog, Hollywood's terrain was traversed by cattle trails, its palm-treed landscape interrupted by only a loose scattering of structures: a few churches, of course; the obligatory Masonic Temple; a random assortment of stores, many of which supplied feed and grain; and a red and green streetcar that rumbled unsteadily down unpaved

Hollywood Boulevard (looking east toward Highland
Avenue) in 1905. Six years later, this placid little cow
town would be transformed into the center of the moving picture industry.

streets. Hollywood Boulevard, then called Prospect Avenue, was a wide dirt road surrounded on all sides by lemon groves; the entire area now known as West Hollywood was a tomato patch; Sunset and Gower, where the fledgling motion picture studios would soon locate, was a vast vista of citrus fields; Vine Street, also unpaved, was shaded by pepper trees; and the Cahuenga Pass, now the hopelessly congested Ventura Freeway, was a circuitous, rocky mountain pass. Traffic then was sparse. Spotting an automobile would have been considered an event; most Hollywoodians rode in horse-drawn surreys or six-mule-team wagons. Aside from a slight aroma of cow manure, the air was clear enough—those who remember that far back say the sky tended to be a bit hazy in the summertime, but on a clear day, of which there were many, you could actually see the ocean.

But Hollywood was growing steadily, and by 1903, the population had risen to seven hundred inhabitants. At midyear, the town's Board of Trade voted eighty-eight to seventy-seven to incorporate; a charter was granted and the municipality of Hollywood was born. This distinction was accompanied by the usual set of requirements, not the least of which was the burning necessity to establish a high school to serve Hollywood as well as the nearby backwater outposts of Los Feliz, Lankershim, Cahuenga, Coldwater, Laurel, and the Pass District, a vast area encompassing part of Beverly Hills and what is today referred to deprecatingly as "the Valley."

Without wasting any time, the new city council passed a school measure, only to discover that they were two students short of the twenty-four needed to establish a school. The countryside was raked for eligible children of high school age, but to no avail; the roster was still short by two bodies. To solve the dilemma a little fancy footwork was called for, and one of the city's real estate tycoons, a Mr. H. J. Whitley, came to the rescue by placing an advertisement in one of the local papers: "Six months rent free will be given any family having children of high school age who will come to Hollywood to live." Freebies were just as popular then as they are now, and by September 1903 the new Hollywood Union High School, as it was first called, was in business.

Unfortunately, there was no school building available right away, so the Hollywood Union High School took up temporary quarters in an empty storeroom of the Masonic Temple on Highland Avenue, just north of Hollywood Boulevard, not far from the newly built Hollywood Hotel. (Some years later, the luxurious hotel would go down in tabloid history as the place where Rudolph Valentino's new bride, Jean Acker, locked him out of their honeymoon suite.) The storeroom had been divided into three rooms by light partitions, which, in the waggish words of one of the first students, "enabled each class to interfere with the others' recitations." School commenced promptly at nine o'clock in the morning and ended at three. Students traveled to and from the "campus" horseback, on donkeys, or in carriages. Those who walked often picked ripe pineapples along the way. After school, students bent on mischief could amuse themselves by molesting the foxes and coyotes that roamed Hollywood Boulevard or by catching tarantulas which could later be used to terrify their classmates.

That first year there were three teachers, one of

whom, Mr. James Otis Churchill, also served as principal. The boys organized a music club and presented a concert to raise money for a reading table and athletics supplies. A wide variety of subjects—English, civics, plane geometry, algebra, freehand drawing, botany, chemistry, physics, German, Latin, and history—were taught by what must have been a fantastically overworked faculty. Two of the three teachers were women, and they received $90.00 a month for their services. Mr. Churchill's salary was $137.50, the extra $47.50 in compensation for his administrative duties.

Within just a few months of its not so grand opening, Hollywood Union High School had grown more rapidly than anyone had anticipated, and the students overflowed into an abandoned bakery shop next door, while the city council debated endlessly on the exact location of the proposed school building. Local farmers, who hated to see good farmland go to waste, rallied against the idea, calling it "a ridiculous piece of extravagance to build such a school in this part of the country." District strife and petty jealousies dominated the council deliberations, and while the students learned their lessons among the baked goods, much time was squandered arguing over a proposed list of names for the new school. Such candidates as Cahuenga Valley High School and Pacific Union High School were eventually abandoned in favor of Hollywood Union High School. A few years later, the word *Union* was dropped.

An equally momentous local battle waged that year concerned the choice of the school's official colors. Some thought Harvard crimson and white suitably dignified, while others preferred royal purple and white. This squabble, which ultimately involved the entire community, became so heated and so consuming that, at least on the social level, it completely overshadowed the national race for President (Theodore Roosevelt versus Alton B. Parker) that was also being waged at the time. (Crimson and white eventually won out for Hollywood, Roosevelt for the nation.) Miraculously, the beleaguered city council did manage to pass one significant school-related ordinance without much discord that year—it required sheepherders to limit their flocks to two hundred sheep because when they drove them down Sunset to market, the noise disturbed the students.

In the midst of all this—classrooms held in a bakery, noisy sheep, and an indecisive, embattled city council—Mr. Churchill and his meager faculty were trying their mightiest to conduct classes in a civilized manner and matriculate their students. At the end of the first school year, in June of 1904, principal Churchill summed up the school's activities in "The First Annual Report of the Hollywood Union High School," a veritable model of forbearance considering the circumstances:

> The students selected their course and entered upon their work with enthusiasm. They seemed to realize that orderly conduct would be especially necessary for a successful year's work. The students learn the principles of Parliamentary Law, reading, speaking, debating and presiding at a meeting. In addition to this, the girls have a basketball team and the boys an athletic association. An orchestra (mandolins and guitars) has also been of great interest.

To this, Churchill added an appeal: "As physical culture is part of our work, I earnestly recommend that provision be made for systematic drill in it next year. Our
boys are round-shouldered and girls hollow-chested and,
if room can be secured, I believe a daily exercise in systematic gymnastics will add to the value of the school."

Earlier that year, in spite of the farmers' protests, a
bond issue had carried and six acres of prime farmland
at the corner of Sunset and Highland were purchased
for the purpose of erecting a new school building. Work
was scheduled to begin posthaste, for by 1904 the school
that was once short by two students had a roster of nearly
seventy-five.

2.

The atmosphere of the school is clean and wholesome. Meanness and vice are not tolerated.
> —From a 1909 pamphlet
> on Hollywood High

At two o'clock one sunny afternoon in November 1904, a raucous parade of Hollywood citizens, led by the town marshal, his five deputies, and a notoriously out-of-tune combo called the Catalina Band, marched south down Highland Avenue, at that time still a wagon-rutted dirt road. The revelers had come to watch the cornerstone laying of the proposed new sixty-seven-thousand-dollar union high school, described by the *The Hollywood Sentinel* as an edifice that would be "the costliest, most thoroughly equipped and most beautifully located union high school building in Southern California." Set in the middle of the wide, barren landscape—the only foliage in sight was six cactus plants, a struggling lawn, and several scrawny sunflowers by the road—the building was planned as a three-story yellow brick structure capped with a silver dome and adorned by Roman-style columns at the entrance. Inside, the new school building was to feature, as its architectural *pièce de résistance*, an atrium, modeled on the ancient Roman design, complete with real marble and a cluster of ferns growing from an open space in the floor.

Hollywood High (top, center) and the surrounding neighborhood in 1905. Local farmers called the $67,000 structure "a ridiculous piece of extravagance" and would rather have kept the land free for farming.

The architecture may have been ancient, but the technology was to be up-to-date, for, as *The Sentinel* reported, "one of the most thrilling features was the electrical system, including a program clock which rang the bells automatically, fire alarms and telephones in each room!"

Actually, the building turned out to be something of an eyesore. Photos of the era show a massive Roman temple plunked down incongruously in the middle of a vast empty field. By contrast, the modest buildings across the street look like a Hollywood backdrop of Main Street America, circa 1900; when one takes in the whole panorama, it is as if two different movie sets had been inadvertently placed together. One almost expects a togaed Julius Caesar to walk out of the nearby feed and grain store and orate his way to the Roman temple across the street. In this respect, the farmers were right: The school building was indeed ridiculous.

Nevertheless, by September 1905, the first floor was complete and the students began to move in. (It would be a while yet before the second floor was ready for occupation.) One early student breathlessly recalled this momentous occasion in the pages of the premiere issue of the school's yearbook, *The Poinsettia*, published in 1906:

> The very first day at the new high school we felt now indeed at home. The storerooms had, after all, seemed but temporary quarters. It was a memorable day when the Senior Class trooped into Room 4 and took possession thereof. It was naturally a sunny room, but oh, how much more

so after it was filled with the brightest, most brilliant class of the Hollywood Union High School!

Another alumnus, with equal exclamatory fervor,
recalled it in this way: "Imagine how thrilled we were
when the first building was finished in 1905. From then
on there were glee clubs and organized sports. The
boys played football, the girls, basketball. Assemblies
were three times a week and there were debates in the
evening!"

A tennis team was also organized, but the fact that
there were no courts in the general vicinity put a slight
damper on the team's competitive edge. Boys' football
got off to a rocky start as well. Once it was decided that
football was a desirable activity, the boys assembled on
the field only to discover that none of them really knew
how to play the game. Two or three would-be partici-
pants had a vague idea about the sport, but they were
not sufficiently knowledgeable to carry off an actual play.
Fortunately, their coach, who doubled as the girls' glee
club director, did know a thing or two about the sport
and, in the words of one student, "offered the boys a few
weeks of concentrated instruction, which seems to have
consisted mainly in showing them how to jump on the
ball without running their heads into the ground up to
their ears."

But athletics comprised only one facet of James Otis
Churchill's far-reaching concept of the well-rounded high
school student. Throughout his short tenure at the
school's helm, he endeavored to mold his youthful flock
into perfect specimens of modern men and women. (In

Hollywood High as it looked in 1905, shortly after it was erected. The building, which was capped with a yellow dome, was demolished after the earthquake of 1933.

Since Hollywood was primarily a farming community before the movies came to town, courses in horticulture were popular. Though farmers didn't wear ties to the fields in 1911, the students did.

A freehand drawing class at Hollywood High, circa 1912. These students are doing pen and ink calligraphy of the school's motto, "Achieve the Honorable."

those innocent days, teenagers were still considered malleable.) In addition to such formal disciplines as Latin and Greek, debate, public speaking, and drama were emphasized from the school's earliest days, and moral values and the nuances of etiquette were also stressed.

Churchill, who had been a math teacher most of his life, had a distinct penchant for order and a pronounced tendency toward the issuing of memorable—if not original—axioms. "Obedience to higher authority," he once proclaimed, "is the difference between the good citizen and the anarchist." And on another occasion: "Don't talk too much. The world may never discover how much you don't know if you keep still." These words he must have uttered with some regularity, for the student body was familiar enough with them to feature half a page of Churchill's more notable quotes in the 1908 issue of *The Poinsettia.*

James Otis Churchill had high aspirations for his school and was probably pleased at the strides he saw it make in the early years over which he presided. But he died in 1909, two years before the movies came to town, bringing with them another kind of aspiration altogether.

3.

Our pleasant task it has been to store within these pages the golden nuggets and bright sunshine of yet another year of happy high school days.

—Foreword to the 1909 issue
of *The Poinsettia*

Educated at Harvard, Dr. William Snyder had been head of the physics department at Hollywood High when the school board elected him principal in 1909. Churchill, though much mourned and beloved, held the job for a scant six years; Snyder would manage to survive twenty, during which Hollywood High made its greatest advances. Churchill had set the course; Snyder navigated through choppy waters. And most of Snyder's innovations—the honor system; the school's motto, "Achieve the Honorable," the service club, the annual Christmas drive, the honor society, and, perhaps most significant, a much-enhanced drama department—endured for many decades.

Snyder, known affectionately to the students as "Doc," was a short, somewhat plump man, described by several alumni as "roly-poly" in shape. Golf was his main extracurricular passion, and he was good enough at it to win a number of local championships. Though a strict disciplinarian, he was known to enjoy a good clean joke from time to time, and those who remember him say that he was understanding and never too busy to counsel a student in need of guidance.

By the time "Doc" Snyder took up the reins, the campus had already undergone considerable expansion. In addition to the first building, the school had a gymnasium and a playing field of sorts. (Sawdust was customarily spread over it prior to football games to keep the players from scraping their limbs on protruding rocks.) New buildings were already needed because the school's population had grown from a roster of 6 teachers and 93 students in 1905, to 16 teachers and 313 students.

The school was now large enough to support many of the standard rituals of American high school life, with a flair for show business all its own. Student dramatic productions had, by this time, become regular events. The first of these, *The Merry Milkmaids*, staged exclusively by the girls in 1906, was a roaring success, and proceeds went toward purchasing pictures and statuary for the school. The following year, the members of the boys' glee club presented a blackface minstrel show which became an annual event—until the advent of the civil rights movement. The debate team was solidly entrenched. (They won two out of three in 1906, their first year out.) In 1912, they decided to call themselves the "Aff-Neg Society," a title that, not surprisingly, did not stick. A baseball team had been formed which won the league championship in 1910, and as early as 1907, enough people had graduated from the school to justify the formation of an alumni association. Their first banquet, held that year, was attended by Hollywood High's first celebrity graduate, described enthusiastically in the alumni notes as "a prominent auto dealer."

Above: Hollywood High's 1907 football squad. Since padding was minimal, the athletic field was covered with sawdust before every match. *Below:* Hollywood Union High School's girls' basketball team, circa 1908. Their ankle-length bloomers and leg-o'-mutton sleeves prompted one alumna to compare them to a "chorus out of the Arabian Nights."

4.

HOLLYWOOD HIGH'S
FIRST *REAL* CELEBRITY GRAD

Unbeknownst to the fledgling alumni association at the time, one of Hollywood High's earliest students was destined to become considerably more prominent than the auto dealer celebrated at the 1907 banquet. At the time of her graduation in 1910, she was known to her schoolmates and teachers simply as Adela Rogers; before long, though, the name Adela Rogers St. John would become a byline familiar to all Americans.

Like many of the celebrity alums who followed her, young Adela Rogers not only achieved a measure of prominence during her high school years, but seemed to have chosen her vocational path at an early age. By the time she graduated, she was clearly the school's most accomplished writer. In addition to winning first prize in *The Poinsettia*'s literary contest of 1910 for a short story called "Measles" (a clever, well-written tale about a group of military academy football players who contract measles just before a big school dance), she was chosen to write the Class Day musical comedy performed by her fellow seniors at the 1910 graduation ceremonies. Called

For the Honor of the Class, it's a three-act play featuring two musical numbers, "The Teddy Bear Chorus" and "The Aeroplane Song." According to the graduation program, the author played a small part herself and sang one of her own ditties.

After leaving Hollywood High, Adela Rogers was signed by William Randolph Hearst as a cub reporter on one of his newspapers, *The San Francisco Examiner.* In the Twenties, Hearst made her a sportswriter, the first female to enter the domain ruled over by such hard-drinking mens' men as Ring Lardner and Damon Runyon. Perhaps Hearst had read "Measles." If nothing else, the story shows that young Adela Rogers probably knew more about the sport than Hollywood High's first football team, for "Measles" is alive with vividly depicted sports narrative. "Hilton won the toss and chose the west goal," one passage reads. "Broadwood was forced to kick and Rowell, their half, sent the ball far down the field. Inch by inch, Hilton fought back to the twenty-five yard line, then lost the ball on downs."

Over the years Adela Rogers St. John would cover everything from the White House to the Lindbergh kidnapping to her own hometown of Hollywood. For a while she was a troubleshooter for Louis B. Mayer at MGM; later she authored a column on movie stars called "Mother Confessor to the Stars" for *Photoplay* magazine (in which she would interview more than a few of her fellow Hollywood High alumni, most notably Lana Turner). She produced enough books to fill a shelf in the library. (In one of them, a memoir called *The Honeycomb,* she waxed nostalgic about her early days as a youngster in Hollywood.)

The 1910 Hollywood High *Poinsettia* had this to say about Adela Rogers: "We knew that Adela was among us from the first day. With all her curls and smiles, she is not easily overlooked. She is a jolly girl and, oh, so clever."

5.

THE MOVIES COME TO TOWN

If the American steel industry had decided to move west and relocate down the street from Hollywood High, a good many of the students would no doubt have gravitated toward metalworking, and Hollywood would be known today as the Pittsburgh of the West. But steel making does not require sunny weather. Moviemaking does. The rest, as they say, is history.

Said history is generally considered to have begun in October 1911. That's when Englishman David Horsley entered Hollywood (by way of Bayonne, New Jersey) with a troupe of forty people, and rented a barn and a tavern on Sunset and Gower for the purpose of making motion pictures. Prior to that, there had been only sporadic moviemaking in the area. In 1903 the Selig Polyscope Company of Chicago journeyed west to shoot a gripping documentary called *The Pigeon Farm at Los Angeles*. Four years later another Selig unit returned to California to film the climax of *The Count of Monte Cristo*, which enjoyed somewhat better box office success than the pigeon epic. Soon thereafter, a number of eastern film companies set up offices in Santa Monica and the downtown area, but it wasn't until Horsley came that Hollywood got its first bona fide studio. Only a few months after his Nestor Studios was firmly established, more than a dozen other film companies moved into the area, occupying old barns or whatever other structures were available. By 1912, Mack Sennett's Keystone Studios was in operation. In 1913, Jesse Lasky and Cecil B. DeMille shot *The Squaw Man,* Hollywood's first feature-length film. That same year the first custard pie was thrown into the first human face. Mabel Normand was the thrower; Ben Turpin provided the face. Hollywood had become Hollywood almost overnight.

At the outset, most of the city's residents were less than enchanted by the invasion of what some called "this troupe of scalawags." Hollywoodians at that time were simple farmers and merchants, many of whom had left the clamor of the eastern cities for a dose of western peace and quiet. The pace was slow, or as Agnes De Mille noted in 1913, "the citizens spent long afternoons moving the sprinkler from one section of the lawn to another." They were a conservative, upstanding lot who had voted in 1904 to ban liquor and outlaw saloons (which explains why the tavern that Horsley rented was vacant). Pool parlors, slot machines, and bowling alleys were strictly regulated by law; the town's idea of nightlife was to go to bed early.

Of course, Hollywood would eventually benefit from the arrival of the studios, but those early days were rough going. Some Hollywoodians refused to let the filmmakers shoot on or near their property and regularly shooed them away. One boardinghouse posted a sign that read

NO DOGS OR ACTORS, and in 1915 the movie companies were banned from shooting in private parks. Retirees who had come to Hollywood to spend their twilight years in tranquillity were particularly rattled by the constant and furious sound of hammering created by carpenters building stages. And the town was appalled when a group of bank robbers, masquerading as a film crew shooting a bank robbery, actually robbed a bank in broad daylight and got away with it, while curious citizens stood around watching.

For the most part, however, the students of Hollywood High were intrigued by the appearance of the movie companies. Suddenly, there were car chases and people walking about town in funny costumes. Also, there were job opportunities galore, for the filmmakers were in dire need of local talent. As destiny would have it, Hollywood High was ideally situated to supply the early silents with all manner of youthful talent. Aside from its location—virtually down the street from the earliest studios—its students, thanks to the efforts of the unwitting Mr. Churchill, were well versed in the formal nuances of drama and public speaking. There were the annual school productions, most of which were sold out in advance and attended by practically everybody in town. There were also debates and speech contests, of course. And on a more informal level, such extracurricular amusements as the annual Girls Jinks, in which the girls would dress up in outrageous costumes and perform skits, and the annual Roman banquet, in which the senior Latin classes would don togas, speak only Latin to one another, and have dinner in the cafeteria, Roman-style, complete with slaves and lengthy invocations to the gods.

The Roman banquet would last until the late fifties, by which time it had metamorphosed slightly into the "Annual Roman Banquet and Sock Hop."

Certainly, the students of Hollywood High were hardly unique in their penchant for putting on costumes and acting out roles. This was considered wholesome fun by teenagers throughout the country in those innocent days and was, in fact, one of the few forms of fun that right-minded parents and teachers deemed acceptable. It was only after the arrival of the film studios that such activities as drama and public speaking took on new meaning at Hollywood High. What had once been fun was now vocational training.

To a degree, student vanity was also affected by the coming of the town's newest industry. Teenagers always have been among the vainest of creatures, but most American teens of the era did not face the daily prospect of being discovered for screen stardom. It is no coincidence that after 1911, Hollywood High coeds began to develop their reputation as the prettiest, most glamorous girls in town, a distinction that would endure for years to come, inspiring talent scouts to attend most of the school's productions, looking for starlets and ingenues. Author Evelyn Scott, a teenager herself when the movie companies settled in Hollywood, aptly described the new self-consciousness that suddenly afflicted certain townspeople: "Most Hollywoodians went about their tasks . . . as before. The difference was that the drive or walk to work might be interrupted by a movie chase or that your neighbor at the weekly sing could be a star. Next week, for that matter, *you* could be a star."

Every year, the school's senior Latin classes put on a Roman banquet, complete with togas and invocations to the gods. This one took place in 1912. The tradition would continue into the 1950s, though by then it would be known as the "Roman Banquet and Sock Hop."

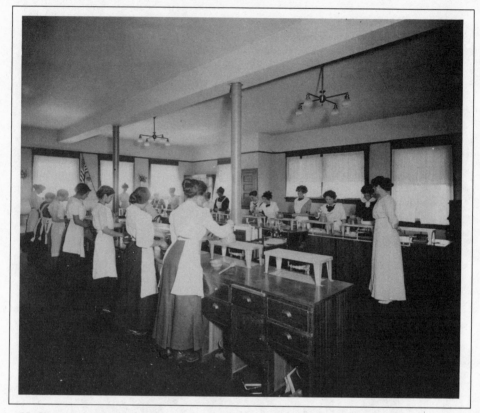

Hollywood High's glamorous young coeds learn Domestic Science, circa 1913.

6.

QUEEN OF THE THRILLERS

Hollywood High's first movie star alumna was Ruth Roland, who practically· jumped from the classroom to the studio lot before the newly arrived filmmakers had time to cool their heels. Her name may not ring with familiarity today, but there was a time when she was as famous as a movie star could be. Beginning in 1911, she churned out one film after another, some two hundred silents in little over three years, and by the Twenties she was widely known as the "Queen of the Serial Thrillers."

Ruth Roland had a head start on stardom, however, her career having begun before the movie companies arrived in her neighborhood. In fact, she had already made a name for herself long before she ever entered Hollywood High. At the age of two, she was performing on the legitimate stage and in vaudeville theatres around California, billed as Baby Ruth. At sixteen, she left school to return to the stage, where she played mostly ingenue roles, until the movies discovered her in 1911. After a series of melodramas, Westerns, and comedies for Mack Sennett, she made her first serial in 1915. She was said to have had one of the best complexions in Hollywood.

Whether or not Ruth Roland actually received a diploma from Hollywood High is unknown (her picture does not appear in the yearbook), but we do know that she began attending the school around 1904 or 1905. In 1930, as part of a special alumni issue of *The Hollywood High School News,* the editors included a lengthy article entitled "Ruth Roland Recalls Escapades as Pupil." These escapades, it seems, had caused Miss Roland to spend a good deal of time in after-school detention, though they were rather tame compared to the adventures of students in later years. "I was seldom quiet in study hall," she recalled for the newspaper, "and was always being sent to Professor Churchill to be reprimanded."

Young Ruth Roland had her own way of escaping the boredom of after-school detention, a technique that may have depended for its effectiveness on the stage presence only an already seasoned performer could call upon: "I used to sneak out in my last period, which was study hall, and put on my gym suit," she said. "Then, after school, I'd just sit and stare, first at the teacher and then at the clock, until he became so nervous, he'd dismiss me."

Roland's favorite pastimes in those days were athletics—she played basketball with the girls and claims to have played football with the boys, though it's doubtful she was much more than a mascot. She roller-skated to and from school and wore her hair in braids. She was also a member of Hollywood High's first glee club and sang a song called "Don't You Want a Little Dog" at their performances. It was her favorite song, but apparently she could never finish it without bursting into tears.

Roland was bitten by the movie bug during a summer

break away from Hollywood High. As the story goes, she was vacationing in Texas when a friend told her that she was the spitting image of Mary Pickford, at that time America's leading film star. Young Ruth took the praise to heart and, upon her return to Hollywood, began to visit the studios in search of roles. It was not long before she was a featured player.

Ruth Roland may have been one of Hollywood's first homegrown movie stars, but she was also one of the first to watch her career disintegrate with the coming of talkies. She tried for a comeback in a 1930 sound picture called *Reno*, and often spoke of returning to the screen in "an old-fashioned serial," but her career was over by the late Twenties. In 1937, at the age of forty-four, she died of cancer. Though she is featured on Hollywood High's "Celebrity List," one would be hard-pressed to find a student on today's campus who would even recognize her name.

7.

"LOOK OUT KAISER BILL!"
—Headline in *The Hollywood
High School News,* 1917

Since Hollywood High did
not have its own student newspaper until 1917, there is
little record of campus events prior to World War I, but
judging from the pages of *The Poinsettia,* the years leading up to the war appear to have been relatively tranquil
ones. If the world was about to go up in flames, that was
of only passing interest to the typical Hollywood High
student, who was infinitely more concerned with passing
English or getting a date for the prom. In 1914, for example, the opening salvos of the European War took a
decided backseat to the school season's most compelling
event: a vaudeville show put on by the men of the faculty,
for which the affable Dr. Snyder donned a white cap and
apron to play the role of a chef. The following year was
no different. As the battles raged and the cannons roared
overseas, Hollywood High's greatest controversy involved overcrowding. By 1915 there were so many freshmen (known deprecatingly as *scrubs*) that Hollywood
High was forced to adopt a dual graduating system—one
senior class would graduate in the auditorium in winter,
the other in the Hollywood Bowl in summer. This unu-

sual tradition would last until the Seventies, to the perpetual dismay of the winter classes, who always thought they were getting short shrift. The fact of the matter is, they were.

To skim the prewar issues of *The Poinsettia* is to remain blissfully unaware that anything was amiss in the world at large. None of 1915's graduating seniors were even contemplating the prospect of imminent military service. High moral character—James Churchill's legacy to the school—was still the mandate of the day. Hollywood High grads were a wholesome lot, with lofty ideals and highfalutin aspirations. A random sample of student sentiment as expressed in a prewar issue of *The Poinsettia* is vivid testimony to Churchill's success. Three of the departing seniors, for example, stated their ambitions in these words: "to be an ardent worker in the public cause"; "to follow a career that will benefit society"; and "to lead an honest upright life."

That is not to say that the students of Hollywood High were all serious-minded straight arrows. Far from it. The usual assortment of harmless student pranks was in healthy evidence. Kick Me signs were regularly placed on the backs of the studious as they sat in study hall; the biology department skeleton was bedecked with all manner of paraphernalia, from cigarettes to funny hats; and a woeful amount of lighthearted abuse was traditionally hurled at the lowly scrubs. One of the more popular forms of mischief was to tie a scrub's legs together and watch him stumble clumsily about. And, throughout those prewar years, the yearbook was packed with jokes and light verse. This one, called "Gayus Caesar," is representative:

Old Caesar was a gay old chap,
He loved to bet on equi,
Sometimes he won, more oft tho
He got it in the nequi.

He even winked (I've got this straight),
At puellas in the forum
And sometimes, yes, he even made,
Those goo goo oculorum.

Whatever their preoccupations, the students of Hollywood High were a spirited bunch, and as soon as the United States officially entered the war, the school rose to the occasion. Hollywood High's mobilization began promptly in 1917 when, in response to President Wilson's call for nationwide action, a cadet corps was organized. It was compulsory for all boys except scrubs, and featured such activities as infantry drills using dummy rifles, patrol duty, and open formation. To rouse the fighting spirit, a cadet corps band was created, and later that year the Hollywood High battalion experienced the rigors of real army life during a four-day encampment at nearby Arcadia. This was probably more like an extended picnic, but the yearbook insists that the young trainees were placed under strict military discipline and instructed on the nuances of military intelligence and battle strategy. After the war, Hollywood High would continue the cadet corps, only then it would be known as ROTC.

Those not involved in the cadet corps—the girls and the scrubs—were not excluded from participation in the war effort. One hundred percent of the student body applied for membership in the school's Junior Red Cross chapter, Christmas gift boxes were collected and donated for the doughboys overseas, and in 1917 Hollywood High supported thirty-three French war orphans. The girls either rolled bandages or knitted sweaters, though one alumna recalls that "more often than not, one sleeve was longer than the other." One thousand beds were set up in the school's gyms to provide housing for servicemen on liberty, and food was studiously conserved in the cafeteria and the cooking classes. A navigation course was offered to instruct boys desirous of joining the Navy. Then, of course, there were the inevitable salvage drives, a popular school activity that encouraged students to hoard scraps of rubbish and bring them to school. As the school newspaper declared, "How is unconditional surrender to the Allies to be accomplished? With men, food, ammunition and ships. We have the men; it's our part to supply the sinews of the war, the necessary material." And supply the sinews they did, with a vengeance. Altogether, the students managed to accumulate 12 pounds of tinfoil, 2,100 buttons, 400 pounds of paper, and 1,200 pounds of magazines.

One of the school's first casualties of the war was the once popular German club. The equally popular Japanese club, formed in 1938, would meet a similar fate shortly after the attack on Pearl Harbor.

War hysteria swept the campus much as it swept the nation. Students of German descent or with Teutonic-sounding surnames were regularly harassed and occasionally subjected to physical abuse. A history teacher, known around campus as a strict disciplinarian, was arrested on charges of being a German spy, though it's hard to imagine the Kaiser being overly interested in goings-on at Hollywood High. An art student named Harold Grieve, in search of real-life models for a war poster, was found snooping around the San Pedro navy yard and nearly arrested for espionage. He managed to talk his way out of it.

Meanwhile, *The Hollywood High School News,* which began publication by 1917, rang with rabid editorials supporting the war effort and carried news of alumni soldiers as well as enlistment announcements. "Bogart Rogers Downs First Teuton!" shrieked one headline, regarding the aviation exploits of a member of the class of 1915. "He downed the German in an air fight precipitated by a covey of enemy planes while escorting several bombers over France." Later, Bogart Rogers wrote to his mother: "Knocked down old No. 1 Hun a couple of days ago and have felt horribly offensive ever since!" Published letters from those in active service overseas provided the students with vivid accounts of submarine chases and air fights. A German military helmet captured by a member of the class of 1917 was put on exhibition in the library for the duration of the conflict. And even the annual alumni banquets were given war themes. The 1918 get-together featured such musical numbers as "Back from the Front" and "A Few Words from Wilhelm."

The movie studios did their part to aid and, of course, capitalize on the war effort as well. America's intense hatred of the Hun spawned a rash of propaganda films in which the Germans were depicted as subhuman ogres whose strategy for winning the war was to skewer French babies on their bayonets. Studio press agents got on the bandwagon also and went to great lengths to photograph their new stars and starlets performing war-related civic duties. One wartime press photo shows an inge- nue standing proudly in front of a massive pile of old newspapers.

Moviedom's greatest contribution, however, lay in fund-raising. Douglas Fairbanks and Mary Pickford bought $240,000 worth of Liberty Bonds. (Their check was placed in the window of a Hollywood Boulevard shop to convince local skeptics it wasn't just a publicity stunt.) Charlie Chaplin conducted a band concert for the Red Cross and auctioned off his famous hat, cane, and mus- tache. Paramount studio boss Jesse Lasky and Cecil B. DeMille organized the Lasky Home Guard, a regiment composed solely of movie people who, Lasky boasted, were to be uniformed and equipped at the sole expense of the Lasky Company. During their first parade, how- ever, the Home Guard aroused the mirth of the com- munity by marching down Hollywood Boulevard in civilian clothes, armed with brooms and prop dummy rifles. In 1918, cowboy star William S. Hart went on a ten-day, nineteen-city tour and sold over two million dol- lars' worth of Liberty Bonds. Mobbed by his healthy con- tingent of fans, who tore at his clothing, he was prompted to remark, "Anytime I'm wanted to go to war, I'm ready. I've seen wars and I've seen Liberty Loan drives. Give me war."

The War is over. The flu has flown. The soldier
boys are getting home. Reunions are in order!
        —Dr. Snyder's invitation
          to the 1919 alumni banquet

When Armistice Day came
on November 11, 1918, there were no students to be
found on the campus of Hollywood High. The school
was deserted, its grounds eerily silent, its hallways deso-
late. Because of the influenza epidemic that swept the
area, the school board ordered all public schools closed
for seven weeks between October and December of that
year, and Hollywood High was no exception. "The cause
of this epidemic," proclaimed the school newspaper in
typical jingoistic fashion, "is laid to the Germans."

Later that same year, citing "health and safety reasons," the local health department decided to ban football in the public schools. The resulting public outcry
caused the same health officials to repeal their ban after
it had only been in force for a week. There were limits
to how much the community would endure.

The flu took its toll. Numerous Hollywood High students caught it. Those who were not quarantined wore
gauze masks and white clothes; white was thought to be
a germ repellent. The flu even inspired one joke that

circulated among the students and involved a bird named Enza: "I opened my bird cage and in flew Enza."

Bad as the epidemic was, it did not mute the area's Armistice Day celebrations, most of which were concentrated along Hollywood Boulevard. Cars and bicycles sped down the street with tin cans attached to their tires, Klaxons blaring, and rumble seats overflowing, while the Kaiser was ceremoniously hanged in effigy from a lamppost. The main event, however, was a grand parade led by Douglas Fairbanks, Mary Pickford, and D. W. Griffith.

By early 1919 the epidemic had passed, the schools reopened, and things began to return to normal. Hollywood High continued to support a number of French orphans until sometime in the Twenties, and there was a marked "Postwar Progress" theme to many of the assembly lectures, but the war was no longer the main event. Track, swimming, and sharpshooting had been added to the athletics roster. The debating team, supporting the affirmative side of such scintillating subjects as "Resolved: The U.S. Government should return the railroads to private management," beat Glendale High, while the student orators participating in the local declamation contest spoke on such worthy topics as "The League of Nations" and "The War Aims of the Allies." The Roman Banquet started up again, a summer school was established, and as usual, the scrubs were mercilessly tormented.

One lasting by-product of the war was the formation of the Ephebian Society by the Los Angeles board in 1918. With "the safeguarding of democracy in the schools" as its purported aim, it was primarily an honorary association of the choicest students from each high school in the district. Ephebians were selected by the faculty of each school on the basis of three criteria: scholarship, leadership, and character. Membership was considered the greatest single honor any high school student could attain. Of all Hollywood High's celebrity grads, only three would reach this lofty height, though fortunately none was ever called upon personally to safeguard democracy in the school. Democracy never really existed at Hollywood High in the first place.

With the exigencies of the war effort behind them, the girls turned to more important matters, such as what to wear. Back in 1917, with the air of self-sacrifice permeating the school, the female contingent of the student body had held long discussions on what the most appropriate style of graduation gown would be. "A simple dress," they had decided then. "It is wartime! We must save!" Money that would ordinarily have been lavished on gowns and jewelry was instead supposedly spent on war bonds. But with the war over, another debate over style raged throughout the school and would continue to rage long into the Twenties. An editorial in *The Hollywood High School News* summed it up best: "A great movement is on throughout Southern California to regulate the dress of girls attending high school. If it proves beneficial and a decided improvement over the unregulated outfit, Hollywood should by all means fall in line and prove in one more way the spirit of Democracy prevailing in this institution." Democracy was a popular word in those days, and it was often misused.

Regulated dress might have seemed a worthy idea to

whoever wrote the editorial—perhaps a prim, studious type looking for brownie points from the paper's faculty adviser—but Hollywood High's more glamour-oriented coeds were simply not buying it. The policy, though debated furiously, would never be adopted.

9.

YOU OUGHT TO BE IN PICTURES

Between 1910 and the end of the decade, Hollywood's population soared an amazing 720 percent, from five thousand to thirty-six thousand people. Largely responsible for this was the motion picture industry. By 1919 about forty million Americans went to movie theatres each week, and the twenty studios in Hollywood—Fox, Paramount, Universal, to name a few—were employing thousands and logging an annual payroll of about $25 million.

As inflated as the industry had become, it could hardly support the thousands of aspiring actors and actresses who converged on Hollywood every year in search of fame and fortune. Many of these were star-struck girls who seemed willing to do practically anything to get a break. (Mack Sennett once recalled auditioning a Vermont schoolteacher trying out for a role in one of his comedies: "When I said 'Let's see your knees, honey,' she heisted her dress all the way and spun around buff-naked.") Fearing that the population explosion threatened to inundate the city with hordes of unemployed actors, the Hollywood Chamber of Commerce published an advertisement in the nation's newspapers and magazines, designed to discourage would-be immigrants. The ad pictured a massive throng of actors standing outside a tiny studio employment office. "Don't Try to Break Into the Movies in Hollywood Until You Have Obtained Full, Frank, and Dependable Information!" screamed the boldface caption. "Out of 100,000 Persons Who Started at the Bottom of the Screen's Ladder of Fame, ONLY FIVE REACHED THE TOP."

No one knows for sure exactly how many Hollywood High graduates started at the bottom of the ladder prior to the turn of the decade, but it is probably safe to assume that more than a few alumni became cameramen, prop masters, editors, extras, scenarists, and makeup artists. Ruth Roland might have been the era's only real movie star alum, but several others made minor reputations as character actors and starlets. Carmelita Geraghty, Class of 1919, achieved a measure of success as a Mack Sennett featured player. In a piece called "Hollywood Hi-Stars," published years later, *The Los Angeles Times* described her as having been "transformed from one of the belles of the Hollywood campus to one of the belles of the Mack Sennett lot." Her classmate Lloyd Corrigan, a popular student who contracted the flu in 1918 but survived it, would later become a well-known character actor, scriptwriter, and director. His acting credits include *Young Thomas Edison*, *Cyrano de Bergerac*, and *The Manchurian Candidate*, among many others.

But Hollywood High's glory years were only just beginning, and it would not be long before the names of its alumni began appearing on every movie marquee in the nation.

PART TWO

TALES
OF THE
JAZZ AGE

1920-1929

1.

Sophomore: "Have you ever taken chloroform?"
Freshman: "No, who teaches it?"

—From the 1920 annual

By the early Twenties, Hollywood had already managed to develop two reputations—first, as the center of the motion picture industry, and second, as a virtual cesspool of moral depravity. Suddenly there were Movie Stars, a homegrown American royalty who earned ludicrous amounts of money for what seemed to most Americans to be easy work. One fan magazine told its readers that Mary Pickford and Douglas Fairbanks each made $19,230.77 per week in 1921. These absurd salaries aroused nationwide interest, and suddenly the public clamored to learn every detail of the stars' charmed and debauched lives. The press naturally acceded to and capitalized on this taste for the tawdry and invented the tabloid newspaper. Fan magazines and gossip columns were soon to follow.

One disaster after another rocked the movie capital. The notorious Fatty Arbuckle scandal got the decade off to a nice start. The following year, actor-director William Desmond Taylor was found shot to death in his own living room, and if that wasn't enough, movie star Wallace Reid succumbed to morphine addiction. All of which prompted a member of Congress to remark in 1922: "At Hollywood is a colony of these people where debauchery, riotous living, drunkenness, ribaldry, dissipation, free love seem to be conspicuous." To make sure these transgressors did not use the silver screen to spread the gospel of profligacy, communities throughout the nation set up their own local censorship bureaus. This posed an intractable dilemma for the studios since no two censors seemed to agree on anything—what would be acceptable in Podunk could be objectionable in Peoria. Without exception, Hollywood's studio chiefs all tried to outdo each other by issuing groveling statements defending their films as clean, righteous,and morally upstanding, but this had little effect. Finally in 1924, the problem was partially solved when the studio chiefs set up the Hays Office, whose purpose it was to inaugurate a production code that would regulate film standards for the whole country. This made matters easier for the moguls, who now only had to second-guess Mr. Hays.

Meanwhile, back at Hollywood High, still dedicated to the ideals of "clean speech, clean athletics, clean life," there was a strong sense of outrage at the bad rap the city was suffering at the hands of the national press. The school newspaper led the way in defending Hollywood's pride with this 1921 editorial:

Many of the current magazines and newspapers have referred in a slighting or indignant manner to the morals and type of people who live in Hollywood. We, the students of Hollywood High School, are proud that we live in Hollywood and we resent these slurs on her good name. Hol lywood is, it is true, the center of the great motion picture industry. Many thousands of people are employed daily in all the different phases of this great work. By far, the larger percentage of these people are earnest, serious-minded folk. . . . The whole profession and the town are condemned for the vice and ribaldry of a few.

Actually, the school paper's appraisal of the situation was, for once, right on target. The town was not really consumed by depravity at all. The fan magazines had simply made the scandals seem like the tip of the iceberg, but those scandals, outrageous as they might have seemed to the nation, were the *whole* iceberg. Hollywood wasn't any more like Sodom and Gomorrah than Topeka or Boise. Most film people were hardworking and enjoyed little in the way of a social life. Dates were usually over by ten P.M., because actors and actresses were expected to be on the set fresh and rested by eight in the morning, sometimes earlier. Certainly there was talk of wild parties, but the rank and file were rarely invited. The fact is, most outsiders would have considered the life of a typical film worker quite boring.

Naturally, there wasn't much that could be classified as debauchery or riotous living going on at Hollywood High, just the usual teenage high jinks. Slumber parties and costume dances were the big rages in those days, and in 1920 the girls decided to hold monthly proms, which were always well chaperoned. "We read about all the so-called scandals in the fan magazines," one alumnus recalls, "but damned if we could find any wild parties going on anywhere. Since the town was dry, nitric acid punch was about the most potent drink around. Things were just as dull as usual."

Nevertheless, the atmosphere had changed somewhat from the idyllic early days of James Otis Churchill. For one thing, the female students were becoming more independent and outspoken. Not only were the girls campaigning to establish their right to run for student council offices, they were bobbing their hair, rolling their stockings, wearing shorter skirts, abandoning corsets, and, most depraved of all, using makeup. The school newspaper was conciliatory on the subject of girls as class officers ("It is only fair that girls should share honor with the boys"), but downright cranky on the cosmetics question: "Segregation is an excellent and effective idea," a 1921 editorial read. "Criminals are segregated. Imbeciles are segregated. It has been suggested here that something of the kind be tried out in the school. A segregation of all the painted-faced girls into a single roll call room of their own, a certain section in assembly and a certain table in the cafeteria, is the idea.... Since the paint is chiefly for the purpose of hiding from the sight of the world ... a heavy scarf wrapped about the face and head would be a superior substitute." By 1926, however, the school prudes had become somewhat more tolerant of the "painted-faced girls," and coeds desirous of smearing their faces with glop were given a special room in which to apply it in privacy, though, as one former painted-faced girl remembers, "if we were caught with too much rouge on, we were sent down to the washroom to wash it off." Naturally, the girls who wore makeup were also the ones at the forefront of the hair-bobbing controversy, and these girls generally stuck together in cliques. In 1923 the girls with bobbed hair were pitted against those who wore their tresses long in school basketball games (the bobbers usually lost), and by 1926 a good eighty-five percent of the senior girls wore their hair bobbed. The fad was short-lived, though, and by 1927 long hair was already making a comeback.

Rowdyism was also on the rise. Enrollment in 1921 totaled nearly two thousand students, a large enough student body to yield a fair share of creative pranksters. One popular extracurricular antic was called *pantsing*. Upperclassmen would seize a scrub's trousers and run them up the school flagpole. It would then be incumbent upon the pantless scrub to retrieve them. Fortunately for the scrub, the area's climate was generally temperate.

Another prankish favorite among the rowdier gangs was jumping on the running board of the local streetcar and pulling in unison until it derailed. Smoking, ditching classes, forging excuses, and the use of foul language on campus had become widespread enough to prompt the Boys League to hold a Clean Speech Week to remind the students once again of the "clean speech, clean life, and clean athletics" of a simpler time which no one but the administration seemed to remember. Vice-principal Louis Foley kicked the occasion off with a speech, proclaiming that "men of real worth do not use foul or offensive language."

Behavior at required assemblies was also a matter of concern. Several times a week, the entire student body would assemble in the new auditorium (which had recently been expanded to hold three thousand people) to hear concerts by such visiting notables as Rudolf Friml or Percy Grainger, or lectures by local professionals on a

Hollywood High's 1924 student body files into the auditorium (seating capacity 3,000) for an assembly. In those days, assemblies were held twice a week and attendance was mandatory.

variety of subjects—including Principal Snyder's annual springtime address on good manners, generally known as a guaranteed yawn inducer. No longer the serious, mannerly gatherings they had once been, assemblies were skipped by some students, disrupted by others. Teachers sat on every aisle taking roll call; the penalty for absenteeism was usually an hour of after-school study hall. The rowdy element was given a stern dressing-down by the school newspaper, which, on one occasion, ran an angry editorial calling the practitioners of disruption "clowns, boors and ignoramuses . . . babies who hadn't the squareness nor the breeding nor the DECENCY to keep from satisfying their own craving for crude burlesque." The editorial was titled "A Plague on the School." The assembly in question had as its main feature a student recitation of Tennyson's "Holy Grail."

2.

"The Hand In Human Progress"
—Title of the winning submission
of Hollywood High's biology essay
contest, 1923

The students attending that "Holy Grail" assembly were probably disrupted by more than the catcalls and raspberries emanating from the "clowns, boors, and ignoramuses" sitting in the next row. Hollywood was expanding, and the sounds of construction were incessant. Not only were new buildings being erected on campus, Hollywood Boulevard was slowly being turned into the main thoroughfare of a growing metropolis. Not far from where the students were restlessly listening to Tennyson being butchered, Sid Grauman was building his lavish, gaudy Egyptian Theatre, an $800,000 architectural wonder described by Grauman as "a temple to art." The year Grauman started building—1921—was the year in which King Tut's tomb was discovered. The resulting wave of "Tutmania" had inspired Grauman to go with an Egyptian theme. And he went big. The theatre's courtyard was lined with Middle Eastern shops and towering palms while sphinxes and columns flanked the stage and the ushers all sported Pharaoh outfits. It was Hollywood's first real movie palace, certainly something to behold, but most of the locals hated it and referred to its architecture as "early Frankenstein." When Grauman built his equally gaudy Chinese Theatre five years later, another joke would circulate. This one involved Harry K. Thaw, the man who had shot architect Stanford White. It was said that when Thaw first laid eyes on the Chinese Theatre, he exclaimed, "My God, I shot the wrong architect!"

In spite of all the racket caused by the construction going on around them, the students of Hollywood High managed to chalk up a fairly impressive academic record. In 1922, for example, over sixty-five percent of the school's graduates were going on to college, quite high by national standards. There were 105 teachers on the staff by then and a host of useful new courses, including nursing, journalism, library science, home design, history of Latin American countries, and economic geography. College preparatory courses were stressed, but vocational training was also available, and shop teachers conducted courses in auto mechanics and repair. Homework was heavy, and proficiency in English composition was a strict requirement. If a senior's final English composition was found to contain even one grammatical error, the senior would be denied a diploma.

Sports continued to hold the most glamour, and a poll of 1923's seniors revealed it as the single most "beneficial activity." Boxing, wrestling, and water polo were added to the roster of athletic activities, and Hollywood High's football team had by this time learned the sport well enough to have more than a few victorious seasons. In fact, it was during the first half of the decade that Hollywood High produced three of its most outstanding athletes. The first of these was football star Adam Walsh, who went on to become captain of Knute Rockne's notorious "Four Horsemen" at Notre Dame. Walsh's 1920 yearbook blurb—"A football hero sure is he/ What greater glory can there be?"—offers vivid testimony that, even at Hollywood High, football heroism was still more appealing than film stardom, at least to the editors of the 1920 yearbook. The school also produced the first high school student to win an Olympic gold medal: The class of 1924's Lee Barnes took the honors in the pole vault. And Solly Mishkin, class of 1923, went on to pitch for the New York Giants in the late Twenties.

In those days, Hollywood High's athletics teams were familiarly known either as "The Foothillers" or "The Filmlanders," nicknames that did not exactly roll off the tongue. When a local sportswriter dubbed them "The Sheiks"—after the Rudolph Valentino film—the name stuck. (Today, even the school newspaper is called *The Sheik Press,* and the dashing image of Valentino, wrapped in Arabic robes, has adorned the cover of *The Poinsettia* more than a few times.)

For the less athletically oriented students, there were plenty of new clubs to choose from. The Penpointers, a literary association, supplied the school newspaper with fiction, poetry, and humorous essays; the Athenaeum Club was established with the purpose of intensifying "interest in debate, dramatics, and public speaking"; a civics club, the Cosmopolitan Club ("to stimulate an international spirit of cooperation between future American citizens and the people of foreign nations"), a French club, a science club, and the motion picture club (which spent most of its time shooting reel after reel of school events) were also added.

Although the school was already quite large, in the fall of 1922, the school board decided to expand Hollywood High's school district, pushing the boundaries to Beverly Hills in the west, Alvarado Street in the east, Beverly Boulevard in the south, and the San Fernando Valley in the north. Even then this was a fairly populous area, and the effects on the school soon proved disastrous. Though eighth graders now attended junior high, within a year of the district expansion, Hollywood High boasted its highest enrollment ever: 2,717 students. Unfortunately, the board had made little provision for expanding the school's facilities. "CROWDED CONDITIONS CAUSED BY INFLUX OF STUDENTS," the school paper gasped. "ALL CLASSES FULL!" The situation soon became so drastic that classes overflowed into hallways and the average waiting period for lunch in the cafeteria was a solid thirty minutes.

The alternatives were obvious. Either Hollywood High would have to be expanded or a new district high school would have to be built. The board chose the latter path, and Fairfax High—alma mater of Carole Lombard and Ann Rutherford, and Hollywood High's arch athletics rival—was born.

3.

HOLLYWOOD HI-STARS

By the early Twenties, the hottest item in town was a ticket to a Hollywood High production. School plays and operettas were held either in the spacious campus auditorium or the new Hollywood Bowl, and it was a rare performance that was not completely sold out long in advance. Hollywood had prospered and grown, but its citizens were starved for serious culture (some say they still are), and the school's student actors and actresses—trained to near professional standards—filled the vacuum. It was widely rumored that some of the local school board members, who received first choice on tickets, often bought up sizable batches of them to give to their cronies as political favors.

The acclaim bestowed on Hollywood High's operettas and plays was due in large part to the know-how of one man: Arthur B. Kachel, head of the school's drama department from 1920 through 1949. In that position, he would mold many of the school's celebrity graduates, and even today those who remember "Kaich" refer to him in reverent terms. An actor himself, Kachel never achieved much fame in movies. Locally, however, he was well-known as the actor who played Pontius Pilate in Hollywood's annual *Pilgrimage Play*, a religious drama performed al fresco across the road from the Hollywood Bowl. The production was an important event on the town's social calendar and inspired one early tourist brochure to refer to Hollywood as "the Oberammergau of the West."

By the early Twenties, Arthur Kachel had taken the school's fledgling, amateurish drama department and molded it into a professional ensemble. School productions were lavish; costumes and sets were often borrowed from or donated by the local film studios. Competition for leading roles became fierce, and it was not unusual for two hundred or more students to try out for a scant half dozen roles. The school's newly formed publicity department made sure the entire community knew of the event far ahead of time, and reviews appeared in all the local papers. A Hollywood High production never received a bad or even lukewarm review.

Naturally, many of the students who participated in these school productions were not motivated solely by pure artistic fervor or even by a desire to stand out among their peers. Many of them were hoping to be "discovered."

And many of them would be.

In all, two major stars and over a dozen minor ones marched directly from Hollywood High's groves of academe onto the studio lot during the Twenties. By 1928 this emigration had become so distinct a trend that *The Los Angeles Times* ran a full-page pictorial roundup on the subject. Titled "Hollywood Hi-Stars," it featured portraits and short accompanying biographies of seven Hollywood High coeds who had either made good in the motion picture industry or were embarked upon promising careers. Among these were Barbara Kent (née Cloutman), class of 1924, who was signed to a five-year contract by Universal after winning a Miss Hollywood beauty contest. She costarred opposite Harold Lloyd in *Welcome Danger* and *Feet First*. Another rising star was June Marlowe, known on campus as Gisela Goetten, class of 1922, who starred in Laurel and Hardy's first film and later went on to a recurring role in the *Rin Tin Tin* series. Julianne Johnston, class of 1924, was a leading lady of the silent era who played opposite Douglas Fairbanks in *The Thief of Baghdad*. Mary Brian (née Louise Danzler), class of 1926, was pulled out of Hollywood High the day she was to start classes to begin work on Paramount's *Peter Pan*. Gladys McConnell, class of 1923, performed in Hollywood High's production of *Mrs. Bumpstead Leigh* in 1923 and later went on to star in two Harry Langdon comedies.

The seventh of *The Los Angeles Times*'s "Hollywood Hi-Stars" received the biggest plug of all since, having recently begun work on Paramount's *The Four Feathers*, she was already considered a star. Her name was Fay Wray.

4.

I didn't realize then that King Kong and I were
going to live together for the rest of our lives and
longer.

—Fay Wray

Long before a gargantuan
primate would hold her in the palm of his hairy hand,
Fay Wray, class of 1925, was the epitome of the well-
rounded Hollywood High student. Today, we would
probably call her a Goody Two-shoes—the kind of student who does extra work and brings the teacher an apple—but back then her gung-ho attitude about school
was considered the norm. "I loved school, I adored it,"
Fay Wray reminisced recently. "I was a good student and
enjoyed applying myself to my studies. There were no
subjects I was bad at, except maybe Miss Heep's phys ed
class, but that was it." Her grades were high enough to
land her on the honor roll (English and literature were
her best subjects); she was elected vice-president of the
popular Athenaeum Club, the school society that spon-
sored debates and plays; she performed in several school
productions; and she was never, ever sent to detention.

By most accounts, young Fay Wray was popular on
campus, but she made her reputation as a scholar, not a
socialite. Every morning she would walk to school from
her home in Hollywood, and every afternoon she would

spend her lunch hour on the school's sweeping front lawn, among the wild poinsettias. Even her extracurricular life was as wholesome and proper as her attitude about school: "After school I would go right home, help my mother, and then study, sometimes until twelve o'clock at night, but I enjoyed it."

Though she never landed a lead role in a Hollywood High production, young Fay Wray did have minor parts in two school plays—Booth Tarkington's *Seventeen* and *The Pied Piper of Hamelin,* presented in 1923. Arthur Kachel directed both plays, and even today Fay Wray credits "Kaich" with having exerted a profound influence on her. "He was an inspiration," she says. "His energy was compelling and he had great authority. He wasn't stuffy or too academic, but a real liberal personality."

That summer, Kaich chose Fay, along with five other students, to play nonspeaking roles in the *Pilgrimage Play,* one of the greatest honors the drama teacher could bestow on one of his young protegés. "I played a kind of vestal virgin who had to carry a candle up a path," Fay recalls. "I didn't have any lines but it was a good experience. It gave me a chance to get the feel of working every night in a production." Most of her studio publicity bios claim that Fay Wray was discovered while performing in the *Pilgrimage Play,* but this was not the case. By 1923 she had already done a good deal of extra work in movies, and as she later said of the studios, "they didn't discover me, I discovered them." Like so many who would follow her, young Fay left Hollywood High her junior year and, as was mandated by state law, completed her education at a special school on the studio lot. As a result, her picture does not appear in the 1925 *Poinsettia.*

The school newspaper did, however, give passing mention to her leave-taking. Apparently, young Fay's sudden departure caused a bit of confusion among the members of the Athenaeum Club, who had, only two weeks earlier, elected her vice-president. The newspaper's account of the situation, titled "Important Meetings Held By Athenaeum," is indicative of the student body's matter-of-fact attitude toward the film careers of their fellow students: "Last Thursday, the Athenaeum Club held two meetings. Both were of great importance. One was the tryouts for those wishing to become members and the other was the election of a new vice-president. Fay Wray, former vice-president, is working in motion pictures, so is unable to fill her position."

5.

Keep out of this film-acting business; your chances are too slim.
> —Alumna Ruth Roland to
> alumnus Joel McCrea

During the flu epidemic of 1918, when all public schools, including Hollywood High, were closed down for seven weeks, a seventh grader named Joel McCrea was one of the few local students not overjoyed at the prospect of this impromptu vacation. A studious boy with an eye to the future, he did not appreciate the delay in his education, knowing in the back of his mind that the seven weeks would somehow have to be made up for. To keep things on schedule, he and his boyhood friend Douglas Fairbanks, Jr., came up with a radical plan. Since all public schools were closed, they would simply have to enroll at a private school. Without further ado, they combed their hair, straightened their tie knots, and appeared at Mrs. Woolett's Hollywood School for Girls, a nearby private academy attended by the daughters of such Hollywood luminaries as Francis X. Bushman, Cecil B. DeMille, and Louis B. Mayer.

Old Mrs. Woolett, the headmistress, must have been impressed by the bizarre phenomenon of two teenage boys actually panting for education, for she admitted them as temporary students. Author Evelyn F. Scott, herself an alumna of the Hollywood School for Girls during that period, described young Joel: "He was a tall youth with a pleasant smile. . . . It was not going to be easy to have on his record that he once attended a girls' school. Probably it wasn't even easy while he did. Down at my level, the shock of his presence was muted and delayed, but no one . . . could ignore the extra flutter of notebooks, bosoms, and eyelashes."

It was at Miss Woolett's that McCrea got his first taste of acting. He played a bear in a production of *The Forest Ring*, which costarred the Mayer and DeMille girls. He took the role, not out of any particular love for the theatre, but as a purely expedient measure. "I was the only one in the school who fit into the bear outfit," McCrea confessed, "so they gave the role to me."

When the term ended, McCrea returned to public school, then went on to Hollywood High for his freshman and sophomore years. (He would leave in 1922 and complete the remainder of his secondary education at a local business school.) He was lean and lanky in those days, almost six feet tall by the age of fifteen, and classmates remember him as being shy but popular. "He was a nice kid," one classmate recalls, "and he never got into any trouble. He was also very, very handsome, and we knew he was bound for an acting career."

McCrea remembers his days at Hollywood High in a slightly different light: "I was kind of a flop in school," he says. "I was studious, but not smart at all. My tenure at Hollywood High was short and unimpressive. Spanish was my favorite subject, but I was never much good at it. I didn't participate in sports, but I did like to watch the football team practice. Generally, I wasn't too proud of my record at Hollywood High, but I always loved the school." Though he was never actually sent to detention, McCrea does recall being reprimanded once or twice by Dr. Snyder.

An admirer of cowboy star William S. Hart, to whom he delivered papers as a youngster, McCrea had no acting ambitions of his own during his student days at Hollywood High and little stage experience while there. If his classmates knew he was headed toward stardom, he himself seems to have had no inkling and put in minimal time preparing for his destiny. "I had a walk-on part in one production," he recalls. "They put a beard on me and I walked in carrying a long spear. Naturally, I didn't have a single line to say. It gave me a kind of taste for it, but at the time I wanted to be a rancher, not an actor."

Actually, McCrea wanted to *own* a ranch of his own, and he spent a good deal of his after-school and vacation time working odd jobs to earn enough money to buy one. Most of these jobs involved horses. One summer he drove a horse-drawn grader for a construction company that was paving Sunset Boulevard; later on, he was given a part-time job by a local rancher named Otis Clasky. Every afternoon around three o'clock, Clasky would stand outside the front entrance of Hollywood High and wait for his young employee to be done with class. "Come on, kid," Clasky would say, "we're gonna start baling."

McCrea owned his own horse in those days, and once in a while he would ride it to school. (His alternate mode of transportation was a yellow bike, a Flying Merkle.) He had purchased the horse, along with a saddle and a bridle, for eighty dollars from his childhood friend and fellow Hollywood High alumnus, Rex Belden, who would later achieve fame as cowboy star Rex Bell. One year, Belden and McCrea put on a cowboy show for the school at Hollywood High's athletics field. It was a huge success and remains one of McCrea's fondest memories of his high school days.

In fact, it was his ability as a horseman and his need to accumulate enough money to buy a ranch that eventually led young Joel McCrea to film work. Being a part-time ranch hand was fine, even enjoyable, but the job did not pay terribly well, whereas professional stuntmen were making up to fifteen dollars a day. At fourteen he began as an extra, but soon worked his way up to stunt rider. In one film, *The Torrent,* he doubled for Greta Garbo in a scene that called for him to rein up a horse and slide into a mud puddle. He received twenty-five dollars for the stunt, and Garbo was so impressed by the youngster's equestrian ability that she asked him to give her riding lessons. On another occasion he worked with Ruth Roland, though at the time McCrea did not know that the serial queen had also attended his alma mater. It was then that the already famous Miss Roland gave young McCrea the sage advice: "Keep out of this film-acting business; your chances are too slim."

In October 1950, thirty years and several hundred films later, an interview with McCrea appeared in *The Hollywood High School News.* "We gather that Mr. McCrea had a little bit of ham in him all along!" the article read. "We like to believe that this hidden quality was nurtured in our very own Hollywood High School, when he was before the footlights for one minute flat, and had his first dramatic fling—carrying a spear across the stage!"

The article, incidentally, was written by the paper's editor in chief, a shy but ambitious member of the class of 1950 by the name of Carol Burnett.

6.

"H" STANDS FOR HEADACHE

One of the more enduring Hollywood High legends that persists to this day holds that in 1923 the school's football team took upon themselves the mammoth task of building the original Hollywood sign. Hollywood is chock-full of myths, so this one comes as little surprise. In reality, though, the Hollywood sign was built by one hundred Mexican laborers who were hired at pitiably low wages by a local real estate developer. The football team probably *could* have done it, but they wouldn't have had any time left over to play football.

It is true, however, that the students of Hollywood High did build a sign in the Hollywood Hills, but it was nothing quite so glamorous or even as polysyllabic as the Hollywood sign. It wasn't even a multilettered sign. It was simply an H, and it proved to be a project that future students, given the job of sign maintenance, would come to regret.

It all began in 1919. That year, somebody with an excess of school spirit and a shortage of common sense came up with the notion of erecting a sign on the section of the Hills commonly known as "Camel's Back." In the best tradition of Hollywood, this notion soon germinated into an idea, whereupon it became a concept. In those days, with rutted dirt roads the only access to the hills, it was a considerable hike up to Camel's Back, and most of the students probably would have been glad to forget the idea, but *The Hollywood High School News*, ever eager to promote school spirit, got wind of it and started nudging. "HOW ABOUT THAT 'H'?" the paper asked only a month after the idea had surfaced. "The suggestion that was made in the Boys League about a month ago," the accompanying article chided, "concerning the proposed 'H' on the side of one of the Hollywood Hills has not as yet taken effect. It seems to some of the student body that it is about time this thing is coming to a head. Get the Hollywood spirit and get behind this project!"

Mercifully, the "H" idea was completely forgotten for an entire year until, in October 1920, the school newspaper, with characteristic exclamatory fervor, once again dredged it up: "The old 'H on the hill' bee is buzzing again," the editors reported, "and the Boys League is planning to see the H a real thing this year. Four clubs from the League will do the work. Each will take half of each side of the H and the team that finishes last (beware Freshmen!) will make the crossbar. Just at present, however, the main difficulty is to secure a site."

Somehow, the members of the Boys League managed to prolong this difficulty for a solid two years, long enough anyway for the bigmouth who came up with the idea to graduate and thus avoid participating. In early 1922 a site was secured and the League held a circus on the athletic field to raise money for the required building materials. To their great chagrin, the circus was a huge success.

Construction commenced immediately. The first H (and there would be many) was made largely of wood. Two thousand feet of lumber were carried a mile up the hill. When this proved insufficient, rocks were used to fill the gaps. The H's original dimensions were forty feet by eighty feet, and it required half a dozen trudging journeys up and down the hill. "It was a big task indeed," the 1922 yearbook boasted, "and the boys now enjoy much satisfaction over the accomplishment."

Unfortunately, the boys' satisfaction was woefully short-lived, for almost immediately after it was erected, the H fell apart. This was due partly to weather conditions and, as was widely rumored, partly to vandalism perpetrated by rival high school teams. In any case, the sign was repaired within a week and promptly fell apart again.

In 1923 the students used canvas to cover the two beams and crossbar, but this proved unsatisfactory as high winds soon shredded the fabric. Dogged in their determination, the League members nailed tin sheets to the frames in 1924, and though this makeshift approach was destined to endure longer than previous versions, student spirit showed signs of being even more fragile than its symbol. "Due to the small turn-out," the ever-vigilant newspaper disapprovingly observed, "all the tin was not taken up. The soil around the H is very soft and black and much of it falls on the emblem dulling the whiteness."

By 1927 most of the tin had fallen off, leaving a

blighted H, and a Tin Committee was formed to periodically lug replacement sheets up the steep slope. In 1930 defeated Polytechnic High School football players turned the H into a lopsided P. They were reprimanded by their principal and ordered to restore the P to an H.

It was, so to speak, downhill from there. The coming of the Depression made the expenditure for repairs appear a trifle extravagant. The earthquake of 1933 didn't help much either. But the last straw was the fencing off of the dirt road leading up the hill by the city authorities. This caused the school's principal to call off all further repairs, as they would now require the students to lug tin up the hill via a two-mile detour. In 1935 the school finally gave up on the H forever.

7.

AMERICA'S FIRST NERD?

By the middle of the decade, new advances in technology had insinuated themselves into the everyday lives of most Americans, and Hollywood High was no exception. For one thing, the automobile was so firmly entrenched in the area that, by 1923, the school's civics club heard lectures about the city's local traffic problems on a regular basis. According to local authorities, the system of roads was not expanding in proportion to the increase in population, a problem that plagues Hollywood to this day. Traffic jams were the result, and Hollywood Boulevard, a popular cruising area even then, featured some of the worst gridlock. Marmons, Cadillacs, Duesenbergs, and Model T's all inched their way down the street, Klaxons blaring.

Newfangled machines were suddenly everywhere, and the students took to them much as today's teenagers have taken to VCRs and personal computers—as if they'd never been without them. The school cafeteria was updated in 1925 by the addition of a two-thousand-dollar dishwasher and a "conveyor belt contraption," both sent from New York City via the Panama Canal. The following year, a motion picture projector was acquired for use in the auditorium. Its dedication ceremony featured the showing of Harold Lloyd's *Girl Shy* to the student body, one assembly that nobody ditched. The middle of the decade also saw the installation of a phone system throughout the school, but this technological development was not nearly as popular among the students as the three automatic malted milk shakers which were installed at the lunch stand.

But perhaps the single most significant technological addition to the everyday lives of the students was the radio. Radio mania swept Hollywood High in the midTwenties much as it swept the rest of the nation. (Americans spent over $430 million on radio equipment in 1925.) In those early days, programming was still primitive—recipe shows and poetry readings competed with such vaudeville acts as The Smith Brothers, The Gold Dust Twins, and a developing version of *Amos 'n' Andy,* but sixty percent of programming featured music. Nevertheless, Hollywood High was smitten with the new contraption, and many students even sat through Calvin Coolidge's inaugural address, which was broadcast nationwide in 1925. "If your family didn't own a radio," recalls one former student, "you were considered out of it. All we ever talked about in those days was what had been on the wireless the night before. We listened to everything." The studio bosses did not share this enthusiasm. Most of them were convinced that the radio would destroy the film industry, that people would opt to stay home and listen to the radio rather than go out to a theatre and watch a silent movie. As *Photoplay* observed in 1925, "The motion picture theatre owners are lying awake nights worrying about the effect of radio on their box office receipts." As it turned out, of course, there was no need for concern, though the popularization of the radio certainly helped precipitate the invention of talkies.

While theatre owners and moguls fretted needlessly, the students of Hollywood High picked the "wireless" as the theme of their 1927 yearbook. Illustrations of microphones sending out sound waves adorned the pages, and call letters were used throughout as a type of code. The introduction tells the story: "The progress of radio so closely parallels the progress of Hollywood High, that the two have been interwoven in *The Poinsettia* of 1927."

The selection of the radio motif turned out to be peculiarly appropriate to that year's graduating seniors, for class portraits show that they had in their midst one William Shockley, who would later invent the transistor and go on to win the Nobel prize—the only Hollywood High grad to reach that particular pinnacle.

Not surprisingly, young William Shockley was a superior student. His name appears repeatedly on the honor roll, and he achieved alpha status in the school honor society, or E.T.K. His scholarly excellence, however, seems to have been directed mostly toward English. Not only was he chosen by a committee of English teachers and class officers to be on the staff of *The Poinsettia* (his field of editorial responsibility was student government), he was given an award for being the school's most outstanding English scholar. As the school paper noted: "William Shockley was chosen by the English Department and Dr. Snyder for being the most original and brilliant English student." Though young Shockley wrote "science" in reply to a student questionnaire regarding future occupations, he was not a member of the science club, nor did he win any science awards. The 1927 Hollywood High physics prize went to someone named Delmar Larsen.

Known by his peers as a studious lad, young Shockley is possibly the only Hollywood High student ever to pose for a yearbook picture sporting a monocle, which, even in 1927, was a tad on the stuffy side. Though the school paper does not show that he excelled in sports or achieved any notable distinction in other extracurricular activities, he did participate in the 1927 Roman banquet. An article on the event lists him as "one of the slaves." That year, as the paper recounts, a little humor had crept into the festivities: "Before and after each course, slaves (14 in all) brought in towels and bowls of water in which the guests washed their hands. The head slave led the way with a flute solo. He was closely followed by two slaves bearing high a whole roast pig with a rosy apple in its mouth. After the second course, a skit, 'Aeneas' Visit to Hades, or Gentlemen Prefer Blondes,' was given. Before the passing of the cup, each guest was crowned with a wreath and slaves poured perfume on the head of each one taking delight in drenching the guests with it. Another skit was presented. It was 'Estre Istud Sic (Is Zat So) or, Broadway Troy.' The guests then all sang 'Mary Lou' in Latin." The details of Shockley's performance as a slave have unfortunately been lost.

8.

Any undue familiarity between boys and girls
does not indicate good breeding.
—From "Good Manners," published
by Hollywood High in 1927

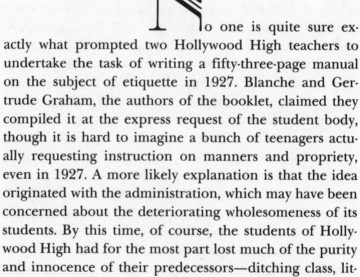o one is quite sure ex-
actly what prompted two Hollywood High teachers to
undertake the task of writing a fifty-three-page manual
on the subject of etiquette in 1927. Blanche and Gertrude Graham, the authors of the booklet, claimed they
compiled it at the express request of the student body,
though it is hard to imagine a bunch of teenagers actually requesting instruction on manners and propriety,
even in 1927. A more likely explanation is that the idea
originated with the administration, which may have been
concerned about the deteriorating wholesomeness of its
students. By this time, of course, the students of Hollywood High had for the most part lost much of the purity
and innocence of their predecessors—ditching class, lit-
tering, necking, petting, and dozing in class were now
commonplace. School spirit was still very much alive, but
a healthy degree of worldly cynicism had set in.

A humorous piece in the 1926 *Poinsettia* called "A
Day in the Life of a Busy Student" described a typical
Hollywood High senior sleeping through most of his
classes, feigning school spirit at assemblies, and spending

every afternoon in detention for tardiness. Graduating seniors were now more interested in making a good living than aspiring to be of any particular benefit to mankind, and more than a few put down "salesman" as their future goal. Inspired by such movie vamps as Theda Bara and Clara Bow, the girls plucked their eyebrows, smoked, bobbed their hair, and put on airs of sophistication. Slang words and phrases such as "hot dog," "the cat's meow," and "the cat's pajamas" had infiltrated student life, much to the annoyance of the English department.

The two Miss Grahams solicited questions on etiquette from the student body, consulted experts, contrived the answers, and titled their booklet "Good Manners." It sold for ten cents. Somehow, other schools around the country heard about the publication and asked for copies. Though it enjoyed a healthy popularity nationwide, its authors were forced to admit that "the people who use this book the least are the students of Hollywood High School."

It is not difficult to see why. By 1927 standards, "Good Manners" was hopelessly obsolete and so obviously directed toward correcting the antics of the more mischievous members of the student body as to have very little credibility among Hollywood High's elite corps of teenage sophisticates. The following excerpts are illustrative:

Loud talking, slang, boisterous manners and especially any action which makes one conspicuous, reflects discredit not only upon the individual but also upon the school.

No girl should remain on the grounds after

school talking to boys, nor should any girl enter-
tain a group of boys on the campus.

No boy should make a girl conspicuous by
showing her constant attention around the
school.

Neither ladies nor gentlemen chew gum in
public.

There are two forms of saying farewell:
"goodbye" and "good night." Do not say "au re-
voir."

In 1934 "Good Manners" was updated by a joint committee of faculty and students and retitled "What to Do."
Undoubtedly, the 1934 students ignored the book's advice as conscientiously as their predecessors. Surprisingly, it was not until 1982 that a satire of this Hollywood
High staple was instigated. Written by a student, Michelle
Katz, it compared the manners and mores of 1934 to
those of the present and painted a fairly accurate picture
of how much times have changed:

PAST	PRESENT
1. A girl may ask a boy into her home after a night out, only if her parents are there and willing to greet him.	1. Only bring your date home after an evening of entertainment when you are absolutely positive that Mom and Dad are fast asleep and/or out of town.

2. A gentleman, whether walking down the street with one lady or more, usually takes the curb side of the walk to insure her safety.

2. A gentleman, whether walking down the street with one lady or more, should switch sides according to where the hooker, drunk, homosexual or bum is. He should protect her from these hazards, but stay away from the homosexual.

3. In no way do boys and girls show their lack of social training more than to destroy table decorations, play with food, or try to attract attention to them selves in a foolish or boisterous way.

3. One should only destroy table decorations, be obnoxious, and try to attract attention to oneself by throwing food when all else fails. . . .

9.

High school students have not reached that age of maturity to be able to definitely define the meaning of God and the universe.

—From a 1927 *Hollywood High School News* editorial

I t was not until the end of the decade that the true spirit of wildness and abandon characteristic of the so-called Roaring Twenties actually invaded Hollywood High. Two events in particular caused concern and anxiety among the school's somber officials. A minor outbreak of atheism was the first occasion for alarm.

Hollywood High had always been populated by the offspring of the upper middle class, families with solid American values and strong religious ties. As Hollywood High was a public school, religion was not emphasized on campus, at least not formally, but it was assumed that students attended church and Sunday school on a regular basis. Thus it came as a shock to practically everyone when pamphlets containing "atheistic propaganda" were found in several school lockers one day in 1927. The student owners of these documents were summarily rounded up, reprimanded, and probably spanked or grounded by their parents. None of the offending pamphlets survives to this day, but the incident caused enough of a brouhaha to inspire the school paper to publish an all-out warning against possible infiltrators in their midst: "Up to now," the editorial read, "*The News* has ignored the recent Junior Atheist campaign, the only manner in which such a subject should be treated. Students of Hollywood High, as members of an internationally famous school, should take pride in safeguarding the name of Hollywood from the inroads of red agitators, atheists and other underhanded organizations."

The second scandal that rocked the school—what several local papers referred to somewhat sensationally as an "orgy"—took place in 1929. In 1927 the tabloids were filled with stories about "orgies" involving actress Clara Bow and the USC football team. Apparently, the It Girl had taken a liking to the college's Thundering Herd, as it was known then, and invited the team up to her house for some fun and games. Neighbors reported that the athletes and the actress played nude football on the front lawn and indulged in drunken displays in the house. Legend has it that Miss Bow—known for her voracious sexual appetite—took on the whole team. The high jinks were brought to a swift conclusion when the USC football coach posted a sign in the team locker room: "Clara Bow Is Off-Limits."

Needless to say, the 1929 high school version of this episode was of a far less sensational nature, but the students who participated may very well have gotten the idea from Clara Bow's antics. According to the local papers, some thirty or forty high school students—some of whom were from Hollywood High—were apprehended by police for holding wild parties at several unoccupied Laurel Canyon mansions. The news reports said nothing about any serious sexual carousing, but almost every other kind of carousing was in evidence. Obscene writings adorned the walls, liquor bottles were found everywhere, and the interiors of the houses were completely wrecked. (One fifteen-thousand-dollar house sustained an estimated five thousand dollars' worth of damage.) Neighbors complained of raucous noises, singing, dancing, drinking, and petting. As *The Los Angeles Herald* said of one of the raids, "Frantic parents, some said to be prominent and wealthy, trooped to Hollywood police station to intercede for 14 high school boys and 4 young girls arrested in a spectacular raid on a pretentious Laurel Canyon home." From October through December of 1929, the raids continued until all the parties were stopped.

10.

Mary Pickford was accompanied to Hollywood High School by her secretary, her cousin, her publicity manager and her projectionist.

—From *The Hollywood High School News,* 1929

Whatever its effects on student morals, Hollywood High's romance with the film community continued to thrive. In 1928 the school's motion picture club was renamed the Cine Club, noting in its deliberations that "the interest in amateur motion pictures has spread throughout the country." By this time the club was producing short mysteries and melodramas as well as assorted celluloid commemorations of school events such as graduation ceremonies and track meets. Like most high school kids, Hollywood High's students joined fan clubs, collected autographed pictures of their favorite stars, and devoured fan magazines and tabloids. Unlike most high school kids, however, Hollywood High's contingent of stargazers had considerably easier access to their screen idols. It was not unusual, for example, to be walking to school and spot Charlie Chaplin or Douglas Fairbanks and Mary Pickford motoring by in an open car. On one occasion, a group of star-struck students drove up to Chaplin's house to ask him to address a school assembly. Chaplin politely declined, claiming that he was not much of a public speaker.

The school also continued to supply the studios with bit players and character actors on a fairly regular basis throughout the decade. Hollywood High basketball star Frank Albertson started as an extra at Paramount and went on to play light leading roles and character parts in over six hundred movies, including *It's a Wonderful Life, Psycho,* and *The Last Hurrah.* The class of 1925's Alice White, often compared to Clara Bow, left the campus to star in such silent vehicles as *Gentlemen Prefer Blondes, Hot Stuff,* and *The Naughty Flirt.* Karen Morley (who costarred in *Scarface* and *M*) achieved a fine record at Hollywood High before going on to movie stardom. Known on campus as Mildred Linton, she was assistant editor of *The Poinsettia,* valedictorian of the class of 1927, secretary of the Penpointers, and an Ephebian. Also appearing in *Scarface,* and destined to play a succession of gangster moll parts, was Ann Dvorak, class of 1929. Jack Webb's *Dragnet* patrol partner—Ben Alexander— received his diploma that year as well. A child star in silents since the age of four, Alexander got his big break a year after he graduated, in the 1930 screen version of *All Quiet on the Western Front.*

The Twenties also produced Hollywood High's first big-time film director. Edward Dmytryk, class of 1926, went on to helm over a hundred movies, including such classics as *The Caine Mutiny, Raintree County, The Left Hand of God,* and *Murder, My Sweet.* An honor student known for his "erudition," he was president of E.T.K. his senior year and earned a scholarship to the California Institute of Technology. A schoolmate of William Shockley, young Dmytryk excelled in science and math and intended to become a physicist. (He placed third in the school's annual biology test competition and seventh in physics.) During his summers, he worked as an office boy at Paramount, where he earned six dollars a week. He spent only one year at C.I.T. (during which he earned athletics letters in football, basketball, track, wrestling, and baseball), then went on to the studios for full-time employment. When talkies came in, he became a film editor, then worked his way up to directing second features. By the early Forties, he was directing four pictures a year.

In 1929 the school got a new principal. On the twentieth anniversary of his term as the school's head administrator, Doc Snyder left to become director of the new Los Angeles Junior College. He was replaced by Louis Foley, Hollywood High's former vice-principal. Students who attended the school under Foley's long administration remember him well. "He was warm, positive, and very visible," says Glenn McConnell, class of 1941. "Approachable, pleasant, and always calm. On top of that, he was a very shrewd administrator. He never disciplined anyone himself. He always delegated that chore to the vice-principals." Foley would serve the school for twenty-five years.

Hollywood High ushered out the decade with a bang by asking Mary Pickford, "America's Sweetheart," to speak in assembly. Though such notables as Will Rogers and John Philip Sousa had graced the assembly stage in years past, Pickford, as the nation's greatest movie star, created a buzz of anticipation weeks before her scheduled appearance.

What made the event particularly momentous was the recent invention of the talking picture. *The Jazz Singer*, released in 1927, had patches of dialogue and a few songs, but by 1929, when Pickford came to Hollywood High to

Long considered the school's greatest administrator, Dr. William Snyder served as principal of Hollywood High from 1909 to 1929. In addition to contriving the school motto ("Achieve the Honorable") and creating an honor society, he was the one who enhanced both the drama department and the school's academic standards.

speak, talkies were widely considered to be the wave of the future. The question on all the students' minds was, "What would Mary Pickford's voice sound like?"

When the big day arrived, the auditorium was packed and, for once, hushed. Miss Pickford, who was accompanied by her secretary, her publicity manager, her projectionist, and her cousin (possibly Hollywood's first bona fide entourage), showed clips of her pictures and gave a nostalgic speech about the romance of filmmaking in the early days. The students were delighted by the performance, and the school paper gave the actress glowing notices. "The fact that Miss Pickford, who has appeared often before kings, was frankly nervous about speaking to an audience of high school students, is certainly a tribute to the sincerity of her character," the paper gushed, though the actress's nervousness probably had more to do with how the kids would react to her voice. She need not have worried, for as the paper continued, "Everyone was struck with the beauty and carrying power of Miss Pickford's voice. The fine quality of her voice makes it certain that instead of depriving her of her present position on the screen, the new medium of talking pictures will strengthen her place as America's Sweetheart."

The paper's prediction was, of course, incorrect. Mary Pickford's acting career was just about over. But Pickford's loss would prove to be Hollywood High's gain, for talking pictures would open up a whole new era in moviemaking. To find new stars for the talkies—stars who could act through dialogue and not just pantomime—the studios would have to turn to the theatrical stage. New York had Broadway. Hollywood had Hollywood High.

PART THREE

THE GLORY YEARS

1930-1939

1.

WALL ST. LAYS AN EGG
                —*Variety* headline, October 1929

For some unlucky Holly-
woodians, economic hardship arrived months before the
stock market crashed. With the advent of talking pictures, most silent screen idols were put through the hu-
miliation of having to take new screen tests. Those whose
voices were too high-pitched or otherwise ill suited for
sound transmission watched in horror as their careers
came to a screeching halt. As legend has it, people would
congregate outside of sound studios anxiously waiting
for the verdict. Suddenly the door would fly open and a
boy would shriek, "Harold Lloyd has a voice! Lloyd can
talk!" Others, like Ruth Roland and John Gilbert, were
not so fortunate, and more than a few hefty salaries
plummeted. The Hollywood Chamber of Commerce,
fearing a catastrophic drop in business, reacted by post-
ing signs on Hollywood Boulevard. DON'T WAIT FOR
THE GOOD TIMES, the signs warned. SPEND NOW,
AND KEEP BUSINESS ALIVE. Though the Depression
would not devastate Hollywood, the good times would
be quite a long way off for most of the community's
citizens.

During the Twenties, stock market speculation had become America's national pastime, and Hollywood's film aristocracy had eagerly jumped in with everybody else. When the bubble burst in 1929, avid movie star investors took a bit of a financial beating, but no one of any note took recourse by leaping out of tenth-story windows. For one thing, there was a shortage of tenth-story windows in Hollywood (the threat of earthquakes had kept most buildings close to the ground); for another, Hollywood's high rollers—those who survived talkies—made such absurd salaries that the crash amounted to little more than a minor inconvenience. In fact, there is little evidence that any of the major stars' extravagant life-styles was especially cramped, at least not right away. The usual lavish parties continued at the usual over-staffed Hollywood Hills estates; nightclubs were filled to capacity; and while breadlines were forming elsewhere in the country, cowboy star Tom Mix—to cite one particularly telling example—spent half a million dollars on a Beverly Hills mansion, paid back taxes totaling $574,000, doled out $18,000 for domestics, spent $12,000 for his fan mail answering service, and bought $1,000 worth of white sombreros. All in the same year. Mix had made the transition to sound easily since his shooting and horseback riding talents were considered more valuable than the quality of his voice.

More important, the film industry seemed healthy, at least for the first two years of the Great Depression. By 1929, most of the nation's movie theatres had been outfitted with sound equipment, and in spite of economic hardships, people all across America were eagerly plunking down their last few nickels and dimes to *hear* their favorite movie stars for the first time ever. While many of the nation's leading industries were reeling head-long toward bankruptcy, the studios were growing fat with profits, thanks to the novelty of talkies. Box office receipts may have been down slightly, but not enough to keep Warner Bros. from chalking up a hefty surplus of $7 million in 1930. As Universal Studios President Carl Laemmle put it in 1929: "Movie theatres are the last to feel the pinch and the first to get over it." The industry would not begin to feel the pinch until 1932.

And neither would Hollywood High. Though the Thirties would prove to be the school's most illustrious era yet, the first two years of the new decade are notable only for their distinct lack of noteworthiness. In 1930, for example, the senior class voted law and aviation the two most popular professions, with teaching, engineer-ing, and stenography placing third, fourth, and fifth re-spectively; in April the die-hard members of the Boys League trudged up Camel's Back with hatchets, mops, and pruning shears to repair the weather-beaten H for the umpteenth time; the Cine Club made a film of the school's ROTC battalion in action; in November, accord-ing to the school paper, "an electric current of approxi-mately one million volts was passed through the bodies of several Science Club members as part of Mr. Wescott's demonstration of high voltage. No ill effects were expe-rienced"; and by year's end, the principal's office an-nounced that 111 students had skipped detention study hall in the course of the semester, with 244 registering as tardy. Six thousand copies of "Good Manners" had been sold nationwide.

Even the ever-crusading *Hollywood High School News*

was reduced to taking up some rather abstract and bloodless causes, interspersed between the usual diatribes on sportsmanship, honesty, and proper behavior. May saw the publication of an editorial called "Overcoming Sensitivity," in which the paper opined that "sensitivity is a disturbing element. High strung people are likely to be less happy than calm phlegmatic individuals." The following month was equally undramatic. The paper ran an editorial exposing what it called "An Epidemic of Fatheads," defining *fathead* as "the term used on the campus to designate an individual who belongs to a small but obnoxious group . . . a person who has been given a position of authority, prestige or prominence, and the experience has gone to his head . . . a person puffed up with his own conceit."

Most of the following year—1931—was equally uneventful, at least from the standpoint of the school paper, which offered no hint whatsoever that the nation at large was struggling through economic disaster. A cartoon club was formed, and the Cine Club made another of its legendary celluloid yawners, this one a newsreel of the school's major sporting events; the big debate among members of the senior class that autumn was whether or not to abandon the traditional graduating capes in favor of light blue graduation sweaters (sweaters won out by an overwhelming majority of votes); and the school paper advised students that if their friends were cross or irritable, it might have something to do with a deficiency of Vitamin B in their diet.

But by the tail end of the year, the first signs that hard times were on the way finally began to sneak into the pages of the school paper with the announcement of the subject of November's debate against Glendale High: "Resolved: The United States should adopt a compulsory system of unemployment insurance." Hollywood High spoke for the affirmative.

2.

Can you fall gracefully? Thelma Babitz, alumna
and former member of the Orchesis Club, demonstrated different ways of falling to the members of the Orchesis Club fifth period.

—From *The Hollywood High
School News*, 1932

y 1932 the party was over.
As moviegoers all over America became bored with the
novelty of talking pictures, box office receipts dropped
dramatically, and the film industry, which had managed
to stave off the Depression for two years, suddenly found
itself facing the greatest crisis in its short history. Warner
Bros.' 1930 profit of $7 million turned into a $14 million
deficit by 1932, and the company struggled to stay afloat.
Paramount was forced into bankruptcy in 1933; RKO,
which had posted a $3 million surplus in 1930, was
thrown into receivership; and 20th Century-Fox was re-
organized. Weekly attendance at the nations' movie theatres had fallen by twenty million within one year.

To counteract the threat of total disaster, Hollywood's studio heads took desperate steps. Paramount laid
off five thousand employees, and wages for extras were
dropped from $3.00 to $1.25 a day (the resulting hordes
of unemployed extras became something of a minor local
scandal); admission prices were slashed, and to get people back into the theatres, exhibitors advertised a variety

of bingolike games called Screeno and Banko, with cash prizes going to the winners. The double feature was created in 1931 as a lure for disenchanted, Depression-weary moviegoers. But perhaps the most desperate measure of all was taken by MGM's Louis B. Mayer—to quell public outcry, he voluntarily reduced his salary from $10,000 a week to $750.

Fortunately for Mayer and everybody else, the industry's crisis was short-lived. A few of the more imaginative moguls perceived that moviegoers would return to the fold if Hollywood offered them something worth seeing. Warner Bros. led the way, producing three spectacular musicals in 1933. *Footlight Parade, 42nd Street,* and *Gold Diggers of 1933* were all huge box office hits, big enough to put the ailing studio back in the black the following year. The other studios followed suit, and as early as 1934, Hollywood was practically back to normal. Money began to flow again and the party circuit reached new heights of extravagance. Carl Laemmle threw a gala bash for the Mervyn LeRoys, hiring a Ziegfeld artist to transform the grounds of his estate into a replica of the Chicago World's Fair. For another party, actress Sonja Henie had her tennis court converted into a New York street complete with cloud formations, and Errol Flynn filled his swimming pool with lotus blossoms.

Taken as a whole, Los Angeles County suffered grave hardship as a result of the Depression (at one point, four hundred thousand unemployed workers roamed the streets), but a few of its communities—Beverly Hills and Hollywood in particular—managed to remain relatively stable throughout the worst years. Certainly, Hollywood had its share of bank failures and bankruptcies, unemployment rose to unprecedented levels, and real estate prices fell dramatically, but by national standards the community remained on a tolerable financial footing.

One of the area's greatest dilemmas during this difficult period was accommodating the thousands of migrant workers who drifted into the state from the stricken Southwest, where crop failures and unemployment were rampant. Known as "Okies," these Dust Bowl refugees set up ramshackle homesteads on the city's fringes, and hobos roamed Hollywood Boulevard in search of handouts. The daily sight of so many beggars practically at its doorstep inspired Hollywood High to snap into action to help alleviate the problem, and a series of school-sponsored charity drives was initiated. In 1932 students, faculty, and campus maintenance men combined their efforts to collect provisions for those hard hit by unemployment. Seven hundred twenty-seven cans of food were donated by the student body for distribution to needy families. Teachers contributed one percent of their annual salary to the cause, and the janitors pooled their resources and managed to come up with $19.74. The annual Christmas drive added to the bounty with 1,500 cans of food, 2,350 garments, and over 1,000 stockings filled with candy for the children of impoverished families. That year, contrary to custom, potatoes were purchased with the Christmas fund money and distributed to the destitute.

Hollywood High also did what it could to relieve the plight of those of its own alumni who were suffering the effects of the Depression. One such charitable act yielded unanticipated results: When former Hollywood High track star George Roth lost his job, Coach Merrill Bailey came to the rescue and hired him to repair the cement border of the school's track. As it happened, the Tenth Olympiad was to be held in Los Angeles that summer, and while Roth was working for him, Coach Bailey encouraged him to go back into training to compete in the Indian clubs, an Olympic gymnastics event. Roth refused at first, claiming he was woefully out of shape, but Bailey insisted, and George Roth went on to win the gold medal in the event.

Naturally, the Depression affected some Hollywood High students more than others. During the worst years, parents who worked in the lower echelons of the film industry were either laid off or forced to accept drastic pay cuts. As a result, some students took part-time jobs after school to supplement family incomes; others simply dropped out to find full-time work. "Things were tight," recalls student body president Bill Lindsay, class of 1936. "Lots of kids couldn't even afford the annual, which sold for only three fifty at the time." Attendance at school dances diminished as well, since the price of admission was a dollar, more than a lot of kids could spare. And many talented students with show business aspirations were forced to abandon their dreams to take up more practical pursuits, such as stenography or bookkeeping.

Then there were those who, like the class of 1938's Alexis Smith, were shielded from reality by protective families: "My parents never let on about the hardships of the Depression. My father sold soda fountain supplies to help make ends meet, and my mother worked as well. But they made my life full and rich and never let on if things were hard."

Though school-sponsored charitable drives continued throughout the Depression years and a few minor funding cutbacks were imposed by the Board of Education, Hollywood High managed to get by without any grave austerity measures. In April 1932 the senior girls decided that, in light of the times, formal graduation gowns would not be appropriate and voted in favor of more modest pastel dresses, unadorned by gloves or jewelry. That same year, as an economy measure, the Board of Education voted to suspend all dance classes in Los Angeles schools since the hired accompanists were deemed an unnecessary expense. As a result, Hollywood High's only dance organization, the Orchesis Club, temporarily vanished. It was later revived, but in compliance with the ban against accompanists, the club's faculty advisor, Miss Heep, beat time with two sticks. The Little Theatre Guild was also voted out of existence by the school board, but the students compensated by forming a drama club. School productions proceeded on schedule—the school board was smart enough not to deprive the community and itself of such an august cultural event—but sets were either less elaborate or borrowed from the studios or local theatre owners. For 1932's production of Moss Hart's *Once in a Lifetime* (attended by the playwright, as well as by Fay Wray and George Raft), entrepreneur Sid Grauman supplied the backdrops.

In 1933, for purely financial reasons, baseball came dangerously close to being dropped as a school athletic activity. For years the revenues earned by ticket sales to Hollywood High's football games had subsidized the school's other sports events, most of them not nearly as well patronized. In 1932, with the local unemployment rate high, football game attendance fell sharply. That,

Arthur Kachel (center) served as Hollywood High's drama director from 1919 to 1949. It was Kachel who inspired such former Hollywood High students as Alexis Smith, Fay Wray, Nanette Fabray, Richard Long, Gloria Grahame, and many, many others.

combined with the all-time low interest in baseball (there were only 250 paid admissions recorded for the entire season, and the team was $550 in the red) caused principal Louis Foley to decide to drop baseball from the roster of official school sports. This was not an unprecedented move—baseball had already been eliminated by a number of other local schools, and by 1933 there were only five teams left in the entire city league.

Foley ultimately reconsidered his decision and a compromise was struck—baseball would survive, but only under a new set of stringent conditions. The Hollywood High team would play only one round, not the usual two; the cost of the season was to be held below $250; practice time would be cut down to conserve balls; the previous year's uniforms would have to suffice; and each player would be assigned only two bats—broken sluggers would have to be replaced at the individual player's cost.

That season, either in spite of or because of the new austerity, Hollywood High's baseball team enjoyed one of its most triumphant records.

3.

In his oration, James Pike endeavored to show
that it is our duty to uphold the ideals of our
democracy as handed down to us by our forefathers and not to let outside forces undermine it.

—From the 1930 edition
of *The Poinsettia*

Hollywood High's first ce-
lebrity graduate of the new decade was not a movie
star, at least not in the conventional sense of the term.
James A. Pike, the controversial Episcopal Bishop of California who became the first American religious figure
to break into national television, received his diploma
from Hollywood High with the summer class of 1930.

His career at the school was exemplary. An honor
student from the moment he arrived, Pike was elected
an Ephebian by the faculty in 1930, having demonstrated
"scholarship, leadership, and character" throughout his
years at the school. He was also one of twenty-six Hollywood High students to receive a California scholarship
pin presented in assembly, and a contender, along with
ten other honor students, for class valedictorian. (He
didn't make it.)

But scholastic honors alone do not an Ephebian
make, and young James Pike's extracurricular activity
record was equally impressive. In addition to being an
energetic member of the service club, he was associate
advertising manager of *The Poinsettia* his junior year, then

was promoted to full associate editor of the yearbook's 1930 edition. Appropriately enough, he achieved his greatest reputation at Hollywood High as a debater and orator. After several years of arguing the negative and affirmative sides of such emotional issues as "Resolved: That the federal government should develop and control her hydro-electric resources," Pike took his speechifying skills on the road and entered the National Oratorical Contest. Early in 1930, he was one of six local high school orators named to the first preliminary tryouts, where, in front of a panel of six judges, he gave a forty-minute speech called "The Torch of Democracy," a vivid paean to democratic ideals as set forth by our forefathers. Judged on "poise, personality, composition of oration, and effectiveness," he won handily, proceeded to the district finals, and ultimately placed third in the Pacific-Southwest Finals, an achievement that earned him a front-page story in *The Hollywood High School News* and a check for twenty-five dollars. All in all, poor James Pike must have given the same "Torch of Democracy" speech ten times or more, including once in assembly when he was vying for class valedictorian. He went on to achieve further oratorical fame at Santa Clara University and was later appointed Episcopal Bishop of California. His religious views—many of them controversial—were set down in a number of books, but it would be through his oratorical skills, first honed at Hollywood High, that James Pike would reach millions of worshippers throughout the nation and the world.

4.

EARTHQUAKE '33

In the afternoon of March 10, 1933, at exactly 5:54 P.M., a whopper of an earthquake, centered at nearby Long Beach, shook the Los Angeles area. When the dust settled, 140 people had been killed, 2,000 injured. Students of Hollywood High, most of whom were home at that time of day, recollected being stupefied by the sight of nearby telephone poles swaying as if caught in a hurricane. A block away, at the Roosevelt Hotel, six of the film industry's biggest moguls were assembled in a secret meeting to resolve the issue of industry-wide salary cuts. Two of the men, Jack Warner and Louis B. Mayer, were almost injured when a large safe was shaken off its bearings and came shooting across the room toward them. Warner and Mayer just managed to get out of harm's way. The safe crashed right through the wall.

Damage to many of the area's brick and masonry buildings was considerable. Hollywood High's proud old administration building—the Romanesque eyesore erected in 1905—was damaged severely enough to warrant demolition, as were the library, the science building, and the arts and domestic sciences building. Though times were hard, the school board managed to appropriate $746,603 for the demolition, rehabilitation, and earthquake-proofing of the school's main structures. The old administration building was the first to encounter the wrecking ball. Principal Foley, a camera buff, recorded the demolition with a movie camera, and until new accommodations could be built, classes were conducted in tents and bungalows.

A new administration building was constructed in 1934. It featured the latest in earthquake-proof engineering and was thought to be nearly impervious to the erratic movements of the earth's plates. Unfortunately, it wasn't impervious enough and nearly collapsed during the Sylmar quake of 1971, whereupon it was replaced by another new administration building in 1972.

The 1972 version is also purported by its builders to be earthquake-proof. So far it is still standing.

5.

A SHORT HISTORY OF DATING

Even before World War I, when school dances and proms were strictly chaperoned by the usual assortment of priggish matrons, and dance cards were de rigueur, the custom of going steady was already well established at Hollywood High. In those days, club pins were the traditional emblems of the monogamous teenage relationship, though in later years these would be replaced by class rings, letter sweaters, and ID bracelets. Boys and girls would get together at dances, early evening church meetings, and house parties, where they would listen to the Victrola or indulge in parlor games such as charades. Young gentlemen enamored of young ladies would be required to call on them at their homes, present their cards, and bear the scrutiny of leery parents. Students were generally allowed to attend shows or go to malt shops by themselves, but strict curfews were imposed and usually obeyed, and a lady was expected to behave like one. Anything more ambitious than necking was considered a serious breach of propriety and engagements were generally protracted and formal. With World War I came a new sense of urgency and, from 1917 to 1919, elopement became the rage among many Hollywood High students. Those who eloped were of course not permitted to return to school following their honeymoons.

Even in those days, not every girl was a "good girl." "There were a few who 'put out,' " says one member of the class of 1919, "and there were plenty of rumors going around school about boys who'd take certain girls into the bushes up in the Hollywood Hills." But by and large, the student body was a pretty wholesome lot, and most boys felt lucky if they had actually managed to kiss a girl by the time they graduated.

Things changed slightly after the war. Innocence faded rapidly with the dawn of bobbed hair, flappers, and makeup. The more brazen girls—presumably those who "painted" their faces and plucked their eyebrows—would ditch school and drive up to Arcadia to make goo-goo eyes at the boys in the ROTC battalion, who were encamped there to drill and practice battle strategy. Though the usual matrons still supervised all school-sponsored dances and proms, dating was often unchaperoned and curfews were stretched. Most students did not own their own cars yet, but licenses were available to anyone sixteen years of age, and with the car came a new sense of freedom, not to mention a private place to neck. Steadies would frequent local malt shops, cinemas, and nightclubs. Dances were held more frequently, some at the popular Hollywood Hotel, a favorite of many movie stars, and evening beach parties came into vogue. Hollywood High held monthly proms featuring "good music, nitric acid punch, smooth floor, and a charming informality." Evening strolls down Hollywood Boulevard were popular dating rituals, as was the nighttime trek up to various Inspiration Points, the most popular of which was a secluded spot in the hills that overlooked Pickfair, the palatial home of Mary Pickford and Douglas Fairbanks. Elopement had gone out of fashion.

By the Thirties, necking and petting in the backseat of Dad's new Hudson Hornet were as commonplace as acne. The most popular parking spot was off the road near Lookout Mountain in Laurel Canyon, a location that afforded a breathtaking view of the city—assuming it was visible from the backseat of the car. C. C. Brown's malt shop on Hollywood Boulevard next to Grauman's Chinese Theatre was a hot spot, as were The Palomar (a dance hall) and the Coconut Grove (a nightclub). Boys pasted photos of their steadies on the insides of their locker doors, and dates were usually made on campus during the half-hour lunch period. The updated version of "Good Manners" strongly counseled girls to make good and frequent use of the phrase "Hands off!" There was some promiscuity and some drinking, but in the words of alumnus Bill Lindsay, "We were still a pretty naive bunch."

Of course, not everyone at Hollywood High went steady—those who did were probably in the minority. School dances were generally well attended but suffered from a serious wallflower problem, which, beginning in the Thirties, became a favorite editorial topic of the school newspaper's intrepid crusaders. In fact, many of the dances were dismal failures, degenerating into segregated affairs with the boys too bashful to ask the girls to dance. In a 1934 editorial entitled "Why Have Dances?" *The Hollywood High School News* exposed the problem: "It is hoped this time that everyone will dance every dance, and that no one will come just to hear the music. It does not look well to see the boys off in a corner by themselves while the girls are off in another."

Though the "Good Manners" guidebook was still available to anyone who wanted to know the proper way of doffing a hat, or other arcane bits of etiquette, in the mid-Thirties the school newspaper seemed to feel duty-bound to join in the effort to instruct the school's adolescent sophisticates on the nuances of proper behavior. "Powder and lipstick may be put on in public," read one such advisory, "but as inobtrusively as possible. Rouge is still applied in secret." Tips on achieving popularity were also offered. "Boys like girls who have lots of girlfriends," the paper asserted. "Seems fellows think any girl sincere and friendly enough to be liked by members of her own sex must be a pretty decent sort." A 1936 editorial called "How to Be Popular" offered a series of dos and don'ts for daters. "Don't forget that you are supposed to be the 'weaker sex,' " it instructed the girls. "Let him open doors for you and carry heavy objects, but don't be the helpless clinging type. Don't cuss in public. Don't be a rowdy and yell and tell jokes all the time. Don't be self-centered. Let him talk about himself for a change." The boys received similar advice, tailored to their gender: "Don't pretend to be a big shot and don't always try to show off," they were told. "Don't be a wet blanket at parties. Learn to dance. Don't be too forward or fresh and yet don't be too backward and bashful."

6.

"You wouldn't kidney would you?"
"Sir, your remarks are abdominal."
"But we mesentery on such trifles."
    —Conversations overheard in the biology lab

By the mid-Thirties, Hollywood High's reputation as a proving ground for aspiring young actors and actresses had spread nationwide. Hollywood publicists, striving to liven up often drably worded studio bios, had already bestowed upon the school such fanciful sobriquets as "The Star Hatchery," "The Starlet Factory," and even "Mecca of the Stars."

So many students and alumni were working in show business by then, if only as extras and ingenues, that *The Hollywood High School News* started printing a column dedicated exclusively to reporting the latest student film achievements. Unique to Hollywood High, "Campus Items" appeared weekly and read like this: "Laurel Feinberg worked in *Confessions of a Nazi Spy*, Sheila O'Malley and Dolly Robbins may be seen in several scenes of *Hundred to One*, Vernon Carter worked with Jackie Cooper in his latest picture, *What a Life*. Watch for Peggy Stewart in the film *Fifth Avenue Girl*. You'll see her wandering around in a huge mansion, in formal attire, carrying a bottle of water."

Naturally many of these student extras and ingenues

achieved only fleeting fame, and the majority of them ultimately gave up show business for more secure professions or marriage. Others went the full nine yards. Peggy Stewart, for one, progressed from wandering around huge mansions in formal attire to costarring with fellow alumnus Joel McCrea in *Wells Fargo*. Marian Marsh, known to schoolmates as Violet Krauth, was plucked out of school when John Barrymore chose her to play Trilby to his Svengali in 1931. Before that, she had costarred in the Hollywood High production of *Enter Madame,* opposite Roberta Semple, daughter of Aimee Semple McPherson—and was a not bad basketball player to boot. Hollywood High's Bernice Gaunt, who changed her name to Shirley Ross shortly after graduating in 1931, played the piano in assembly and won acclaim in school operettas. Today she's better known to movie fans for her rendition of "Thanks for the Memory" with Bob Hope in *The Big Broadcast of 1938*. Leslie Brooks (née Lorraine Gettman), whose credits include *Yankee Doodle Dandy* and *The Ziegfeld Girls*, majored in algebra and English at Hollywood High and sang with the school's glee club, as did her classmate, Betty McLaughlin, who changed her name to Sheila Ryan and became a leading lady in such Forties films as *Something for the Boys* and *Caged Fury*. Only four years after receiving her diploma, Susan Peters (née Carnahan) grabbed an Academy Award nomination for her role in *Random Harvest*. Alan Hale, Jr., who later played the Skipper on TV's *Gilligan's Island*, was known around campus as a good-humored, happy-go-lucky guy who went steady with his future wife all through school. Announcer Jack Smith graduated in 1932, and director Earl Bellamy, who directed *Part 2, Walking Tall*, received his diploma in 1935. Judge Joseph Wapner, who presides over TV's *The People's Court,* wanted to be an actor when he attended Hollywood High in the late Thirties but opted for a more secure legal career; character actor Jack Kruschen, whose credits include *The Apartment* and *The Unsinkable Molly Brown* as well as numerous TV roles, was a member of 1938's senior class, and June Carlson, who acted in a few Andy Hardy films, graduated the following year. The class of 1930's Frank Keller won an Academy Award in 1968 for his editing work on the film *Bullitt.*

But the key year in Hollywood High's history is 1936. For it was at various times during that memorable year that Judy Garland, Lana Turner, Mickey Rooney, Marge Champion, Alexis Smith, and Nanette Fabray all passed through the school's crowded corridors.

Would you like to know a pleasant sensation?
Drive your first car fast down an open road with
the top down, and Lana Turner sitting beside you,
holding on and urging you to go slower."

—Mickey Rooney

Shortly after the movies
came to town, the state of California enacted strict laws
governing the education of school-age boys and girls under contract to the studios. The kids could work in motion pictures just as long as their educations continued
uninterrupted. Thus, while shooting a picture, the young
contract players would be required to attend an on-the-
lot school or receive instruction from a certified tutor.
Between productions, they would attend one of the local
schools until called upon by their bosses to resume work.

Mickey Rooney, who had already achieved a fair measure of stardom by 1936, attended a number of schools,
one of which was Hollywood High. (He also attended
Ma Lawlor's School, Fairfax High, and MGM's famous "Little Red Schoolhouse.") His sojourn at Hollywood High
was brief but memorable. Around the campus he was
generally known as a friendly, happy-go-lucky guy who
seemed to like everybody, much like his screen persona.
He used to drive his big, bright-blue Ford convertible
right onto the schoolyard lawn, an act that usually attracted a gaggle of fair coeds who would ooh and ahh

and lavish the seventeen-year-old with girlish attention.

As for scholastic achievement, young Mickey Rooney just managed to squeak through. One of his high school teachers, interviewed by *The Saturday Evening Post* in 1947, remembered the diminutive actor as an average student, tall on aptitude but short on application: "The first thing he did every morning when he came to class was to measure himself against me, to see whether he had grown during the night. Like most movie children, he was a spoiled brat. The only way I could get him to do anything distasteful to him, such as homework, was to tell him he was acting like a child. Then he'd tear through any assignment. Mickey was just an average student with a prodigious memory. That's how he passed exams."

But it was not Hollywood High's academic reputation that attracted Mickey Rooney to the school. It was Hollywood High's female population. More specifically, it was one particular member of that population.

Her full name was Julia Jean Turner, but everyone just called her Judy in those days. Following the death of her father, she had emigrated from San Francisco to Hollywood with her mother in January 1936 and, at the age of fifteen, enrolled in the sophomore class of Hollywood High. She would attend the school for a mere six weeks before being snapped up by the studios, but none of her classmates would ever forget her.

What was unforgettable about young Judy Turner was her dazzling beauty, particularly her silken auburn hair and shapely figure. Even today her high school class-mates (including several famous ones) remember her with awe. "The first time I saw her," Mickey Rooney wrote in his autobiography, "I saw what millions of people were later to see: poise, a superb figure, and that beautiful, innocent know-it-all face. My eyes bugged. Lana Turner was the belle of Hollywood High."

"She was the most incredibly beautiful girl we had ever seen," Nanette Fabray, class of 1938, later remarked. "Even the teachers would stare at her. She'd walk down the hall, looking straight ahead, while all the other kids gawked at her. She was only fifteen but even then she had the bearing of a princess. We all knew she would be a movie star."

And Alexis Smith adds: "It was quite incredible. We were a student body of about twenty-five hundred, a lot of kids, but within a week of Lana's first day there was already talk about the new girl, how gorgeous she was. She caused quite a sensation. She'd only been there a week or so and was already going out with the handsome president of the student body."

Unlike many of her classmates, Judy Turner had not yet decided on a movie career. "We did not go to Hollywood with the slightest notion of putting me in motion pictures," Lana Turner wrote some time later in the *Woman's Home Companion*. "I had no such dream. It would have seemed absurd. I had never acted, I had never danced, or tried to do either." She had been a cheerleader and a member of the softball team in high school in San Francisco. She had even excelled in English, Spanish, and Latin there, but she had never participated in a school play or undergone any training in speaking or elocution. She did try out for a minor role in one of Hollywood High's renowned productions that winter, but Mr. Kachel must have found her abilities lacking, for the role was given to someone else. Which is just as well, for had Judy Turner gotten the part, Hollywood might have been deprived of one of its most enduring legends: the discovery of Lana Turner.

It was her profound distaste for typing that led to her serendipitous "discovery" one winter afternoon in 1936. "One of the horrors I endured as part of my faltering and slipshod education was typing," Lana Turner later wrote. "Somebody once compared my typing to the eccentricities of a balky threshing machine in a high wind. My attack was fast but my accuracy was deplorable." Her classmate Cyrille Block was given the task of helping her decipher the keyboard. "She started the course late and didn't know where anything was on the keyboard. But she was very nice about it and picked it up pretty fast." Another alumna who recalls Judy Turner's brief tenure at Hollywood High is Lois Barthelmess. Lois and her family lived in Judy Turner's apartment building, and it was Lois who walked the new sophomore to school her first day, and who would soon be present at an even more momentous event. "She was totally unaffected by her beauty, but she loved to flirt," Lois recounted. "She wore sweaters and skirts mostly, but no show-off stuff. She didn't need to show off—she was a natural beauty. Sometimes we used to go off and smoke cigarettes on the sly. I was with her when she was discovered. She was a pretty naive kid and very surprised when Mr. Wilkerson approached her."

That winter, ditching class had become so rampant at Hollywood High that the school paper felt called upon to remind students that "pupils must not leave the grounds between arrival at school and dismissal from school without the permission of the office." But Judy Turner's distaste for typing was great enough for her to ignore the warnings and head across Highland Avenue to a malt shop known as the Top Hat Cafe (not, as legend has it, to Schwab's). There she plunked down her nickel lunch money, ordered a Coke (not the chocolate malted that legend has supplied her), and, to make a long story short, attracted the attention of Billy Wilkerson, publisher of *The Hollywood Reporter*, who came over and uttered the phrase, "Would you like to be in pictures?" The students of Hollywood High did not see much of young Judy Turner after that, and the Top Hat Cafe, already a popular hangout for the student body's more urbane class ditchers, became even more popular.

It was, in fact, at the Top Hat Cafe that Mickey Rooney had first laid eyes on Judy Turner one day after school in 1936, a few weeks before her discovery. He was immediately smitten. "The malt shop was a social club," he recalled. "Everyone congregated there, including Lana. In fact, when Lana was there, everyone congregated around Lana." Rooney also wrote that he dated Lana that year for a period of three or four months. They would go to movies, out to dinner, or dancing. "What was it like dating Lana Turner when I was seventeen years old? Did you ever date the prettiest girl in school when you were seventeen years old?" In *her* autobiography, Lana Turner denies that she ever dated Mickey Rooney. But Lois Barthelmess recalls two occasions when she, Mickey Rooney, and Judy Turner double-dated. "Once we all went to a show together, and another time we visited Mickey's father in the hospital," she says.

Another girl Mickey Rooney dated during this period

was Judy Garland, who attended Hollywood High for part of her sophomore year in 1936. She had made only one film by this time, the forgettable *Pigskin Parade*, but she would soon be called back to the MGM lot to begin work on *Broadway Melody of 1938, Love Finds Andy Hardy* (co-starring Rooney and Lana Turner), and *The Wizard of Oz*. It was in between these pictures that she attended classes at Hollywood High.

She had considerably less impact than Lana on her fellow students. In fact, only a few of her classmates remember her. "She was a tiny little girl," one alumna recalls, "sweet as can be, always friendly, never a show-off, and full of fun." Her academic record was not remarkable, but she was known to be a diligent student. Her days at Hollywood High were happy ones, and apparently meant a lot to her.

Though she completed most of her high school education at the famous Little Red Schoolhouse on the MGM lot (with Rooney, Turner, and Ava Gardner), Judy Garland desperately wanted to attend graduation ceremonies with her class at Hollywood High. Ordinarily, teenage contract players would take high school equivalency exams and receive a diploma in the mail from a local high school. But for sentimental reasons, the notion of actually receiving her sheepskin in the normal way thrilled young Judy, and when *The Wizard of Oz* was completed during what would have been her senior year, she bought a graduation dress especially for the occasion. "Isn't it marvelous! I'm going to graduate with a class!" she told her *Oz* costar Margaret Hamilton (who played the Wicked Witch of the West). Unfortunately, Judy would never walk down the aisle with her Hollywood

High compatriots, because of a scheduling conflict. The studio had booked her for a promotional tour, and she was to spend graduation day on the road. Maggie Hamilton lodged a protest with the studio on Judy's behalf, but the MGM publicity department was adamant. She eventually received a high school diploma in the mail from University High.

8.

Alexis Smith gave an excellent account of herself
at Redlands by winning second place in the State
Declamation Contest. She then went to Ohio for
the national contest where she gave the last scene
from Maxwell Anderson's *Elizabeth the Queen*.
                              —From *The Poinsettia*, 1938.

Lana Turner's chance dis-
covery at the Top Hat Cafe and subsequent meteoric rise
to stardom must surely have irked many of her classmates who were struggling to develop their show business careers in more traditional ways. (One alumna has
even suggested that Lana was planted in the school as a
studio publicity stunt, but this is doubtful.) Basically, Hollywood High provided three showcases for its young stars-
to-be. One, of course, was the drama group that staged
the school's popular productions. Another was the Orchesis Club, which put on dance shows and instructed its
members in the nuances of choreography. (The success
of movie musicals in the mid-Thirties made the Orchesis
Club's young hoofers particularly interesting to the studios' talent scouts.) The third, and probably least effective in providing the right kind of visibility, was
participation in one of the school's public speaking clubs,
which could lead to exposure in various local and national oratorical and declamation contests.

During their tenures at Hollywood High, Marge
Champion (class of summer, 1936), Nanette Fabray (win-

133

ter, 1938), and Alexis Smith (summer, 1938) were the ranking stars in all three of these highly competitive activities. Unlike Turner, Rooney, and Garland, they were true alumni of Hollywood High—all three spent their entire high school careers there and graduated in the traditional way with their respective classes.

Marge Champion was an upperclassman when Alexis Smith and Nanette Fabray began their sophomore years at Hollywood High. In those days her name was Marjorie Belcher, and she was the daughter of one of Hollywood's first film choreographers, Ernest Belcher, who operated a local dance school when not working in pictures. One of Ernest Belcher's best pupils in the early Thirties was a young boy by the name of Gower Champion.

Marjie and Gower had attended Bancroft Junior High together (they sat next to each other in history class) and had been partners in her father's dance class. They dated intermittently when Gower was at Fairfax High and Marjie at Hollywood, but it would not be until after World War II that they would team up professionally and become the so-called "dancing darlings of the cinema." Gower left Fairfax during his senior year to pursue his dancing career, but Marjie stayed on at Hollywood High. It was there that she would hone her acting, singing, and dancing talents to a fine edge.

Everyone knew she could dance, but her singing ability came as a surprise, even to Mr. Kachel, who discovered it by accident. As the story goes, Kaich had been strolling the school's corridors when he heard the alluring lilt of a voice coming from the glee club practice room. When he entered to investigate, he was somewhat astonished to find young Marjie Belcher crooning. "Can Marjie Belcher sing, too?" he asked.

Classmates remember Marjie Belcher as being "personable" and "cute." "She was a popular girl and went to most school dances," says Bill Lindsay, a member of her class. "I remember some of the kids used to kid her by saying her father was 'an earnest belcher.' She was my campaign manager when I ran for student council president, and I won."

Though there is no record of her scholastic achievements (her name does not appear on any published honor rolls, but classmates claim she was a good student), Marjie Belcher is well remembered for her many extra-curricular activities. Naturally, she was a regular participant in all Orchesis Club performances, as both a dancer and a choreographer. During her senior year, so much of her time was taken up working on Hollywood High's spring operetta, *The Red Mill*, by Victor Herbert, that it's a wonder she graduated. In addition to cocreating and codirecting all the play's dance numbers, she also took on the role of Tina, a part that called for her to sing as well as perform the production's only dance solo, a waltz. The school paper gave her glowing notices: "Marjorie Belcher won the hearts of every audience with her charming portrayal of the barmaid Tina as well as her lovely waltz number. Her gracefulness made her a joy to watch." Somehow she even found the time to engage in nontheatrical activities. Her junior year, she was elected vice-president of the Junior Auxiliary, a philanthropic organization.

Following graduation, Marjorie Belcher was hired by

Walt Disney to provide the live model for Snow White in the animated feature *Snow White and the Seven Dwarfs*. (Another Hollywood High alumna, Adriana Caselotti, provided the voice.) Two years after graduation she was dancing before the cameras in the 1939 release *The Story of Vernon and Irene Castle*. In 1944 she returned to the campus to perform as guest soloist in a special Orchesis Club program.

Also prominent in the Orchesis Club during Marjie Belcher's senior year was Alexis Smith. Though she was only a sophomore at the time, young Alexis collaborated with Marjie on all the dance numbers for *The Red Mill*. (She also played a minor role and danced in the operetta's tarantella number.) In all, Alexis and Marjie tap-danced together twice in Orchesis Club recitals that year. "I was very impressed with Marjie," Alexis has said. "She was so glamorous and so talented. Because of her dancing, she had already had some celebrity before she even came to Hollywood High."

A year after Marjie Belcher graduated, Alexis was elected to the Orchesis Club's board of directors, and by her senior year she was the club's president. She found two teachers—the Orchesis Club's Miss Heep and the drama department's Mr. Kachel—particularly inspiring: "Miss Heep was a big influence on all her students," Alexis recalls. "She was very interested in the arts, and her interest went beyond teaching. Mr. Kachel was unquestionably the finest drama teacher in town. He was wonderful with inspiring young people in serious drama and he was responsible for my going to City College, which at the time had an exceptional drama department."

Alexis Smith, class of 1938, came close to winning a national oratorical contest her senior year.

Classmates remember Alexis as being nice once you got to know her but a little bashful. Others saw her as being very single-minded about her art. Alexis's own appraisal is a bit darker than that of her classmates: "I was socially inept in high school and had a terrible inferiority complex. My upbringing was Scotch-Presbyterian and I wasn't allowed to date until I was sixteen, and even then my dad would drive me and pick me up. All of my accomplishments—dancing, acting, playing the piano—didn't really seem like accomplishments then. I wasn't popular—I was too tall, too skinny, and not very pretty. I was always in the shadow of the pretty girls on campus."

Though not the recipient of any scholastic achievement awards, young Alexis was an excellent student and maintained a fairly high grade average. She liked French and history best, but was never too fond of math or typing—though, unlike Judy Turner, she considered typing a necessary hedge against future disappointment. "I took typing because I decided it might be a good idea to do something practical, just in case. I think my best was thirty words per minute with five mistakes." A crowded schedule of extracurricular activities, in addition to dance and piano lessons, left her no time for sports. In 1938 she performed a soft-shoe tap dance at a recital held at Fairfax High School, and later that same year created and directed a ballet rendition of a Strauss waltz for an assembly program. In addition to her collaborative efforts with Marjie Belcher in *The Red Mill*, she also appeared in Hollywood High productions of *Sweethearts* and *The Fortune Teller*.

But Alexis Smith's most outstanding high school accomplishment occurred during her senior year when she participated in the dramatic reading competition of the State Declamation Contest. Each contestant was required to give a speech lasting somewhere between seven and ten minutes in length. Alexis chose the last scene from Maxwell Anderson's *Elizabeth the Queen,* in which Elizabeth orders the execution of Lord Essex. She played both parts and recalls being "very nervous." The winner of the national finals would go to the White House and meet President Roosevelt.

Young Alexis placed second in the state finals and was sent by train to Wooster, Ohio, to compete on the national level. Though times were hard, the school managed to raise enough money for two train tickets—one for Alexis and one for her mother. During the journey, the young orator sent regular progress reports back to the school, many of which were read aloud to the drama classes and published in the school paper. In her first such missive, mailed from Salt Lake City, Alexis declared that "Every time I get out of my berth, I bang my head and by the time I get home I will have a swelled head, win or lose."

Unfortunately, she did not return victorious, having only placed in the national semifinals, and was heartbroken over letting her classmates down. "When we returned, the high school band was there to meet us in Pasadena, and I didn't want to get off the train, because I hadn't won; I wanted to stay on until the next stop. My father finally talked me into getting off." Nevertheless, the school honored her with a special assembly, and the 1938 yearbook staff chose her as one of twelve outstanding students in her class to "achieve the honorable." Moreover, a talent agent had seen her speak and was impressed enough to ask her to take a screen test. She did, but the agent never called back. She was heartbroken until years later, when she discovered that her father had secretly intervened, insisting that his daughter finish her education before venturing into show business. Which she did. But by 1941 she was acting regularly in films, and her credits include such classics as *Gentleman Jim, Rhapsody in Blue, Night and Day,* and *The Young Philadelphians.*

Though Alexis's rendition of the last scene of *Elizabeth the Queen* helped launch her on her career, it would be her classmate and sometime rival, Nanette Fabray, who ended up starring in the 1939 film *Elizabeth and Essex.* Fabray (whose real last name was spelled Fabares) was often the one who got the plum roles in Hollywood High's big productions between 1936 and 1938. If Marjie Belcher and Alexis Smith were the school's star hoofers, Nanette was Hollywood High's brightest stage player.

Of course, young Nanette had had a considerable head start on Marjie and Alexis, having been a player in the acting game long before registering at Hollywood High. Her mother, who had dabbled in amateur dramatics and once won a silver cup for dancing the cakewalk at a charity ball, had abandoned her own dreams of stardom and invested all her efforts into developing her daughter's acting career. At three, little Nanette could tap-dance proficiently; at four, she was working the vaudeville circuit with the likes of Ben Turpin (who taught her, among other things, how to cross her eyes at will); and by eight, she'd appeared in several *Our Gang* comedies, billed as Baby Nan.

In spite of her acting experience, young Nanette Fa-

bray was not entirely convinced that show business was
to be her future vocation. In fact, upon entering Hollywood High she toyed briefly with the notion of becoming a doctor. But Hollywood High's drama department
knew a ringer when it saw one, and Nanette soon found
herself a star of the school's stage. In June 1937 she
danced in a student amateur assembly, and later that
same year played the title role in an Armistice Day play
called *The Golden Lady* (in which she beseeched the Statue
of Liberty to let her see her fallen son one more time).
During her senior year, she was chosen for the starring
role in the Hollywood High production of *Who Killed
Cock Robin,* a murder mystery. Her ablest competitor for
the part was none other than Alexis Smith.

Young Nanette Fabray was also active in show business outside of school. During her three years at Hollywood High, she performed on Sid Caesar's radio show,
took bit parts in motion pictures, was a member of the
radio cast of *Show Boat,* and participated in productions
put on by the Studio Little Theatre Guild.

Though Nanette Fabray claims that she was a shy
youngster and had only a "couple of friends" at Hollywood High, classmate Cyrille Block remembers her as a
"lovely, happy girl you couldn't help but like," and Bill
Lindsay says she was "a levelheaded, down-to-earth, gen-
uinely nice person who was never affected by her success." Her grades were not outstanding—far from it.
Years later, she would discover that her scholastic problems were largely caused by ososclerosis (a congenital
disease characterized by progressive deafness due to a
hardening of the small bones in the ear). "I went through
life thinking I was dumb," she confessed in a magazine

141

interview. "I only squeaked through Hollywood High School, and was allowed to graduate with my class by taking a bunch of remedial courses in subjects I had flunked. I didn't know that I had a hearing problem and consequently missed out on class lectures."

Nanette Fabray graduated with the winter class of 1938, listing "dramatics" as her favorite course and "actress" as her future vocation. None of her schoolmates ever doubted that she would achieve her goal.

9.

Temporary hard water may be softened by beating it.

> —From a series of test "boners"
> collected by a Hollywood High
> science teacher

If Hollywood High was the most famous high school in America, that was solely because of the prodigious number of stars and starlets who passed through its hallways on their way to show business renown. But what was the general attitude of the student body toward the school's considerable crop of incipient celebrities? Certainly there was some jealousy, particularly on the part of the less successful contenders, those who had the dreams but lacked either the talent or the good fortune. Several alumni confess to having felt star-struck in the presence of the school's celestial talents, while others shrug and to this day profess indifference, bordering on downright boredom. (One deadpan alumnus has gotten a lot of mileage out of telling people that he was the only member of his class who never had a screen test.) Though the school newspaper appreciated the phenomenon enough to publish weekly status bulletins on the school's aspiring screen hopefuls, it also listed as one of the four biggest "Annoyances" those "would-be actors and actresses who don't know the opera is over." In other words, Hollywood High's student celebs would be tolerated, even appreciated, so long as they did not become the "fatheads" the school newspaper had found it necessary to editorialize against. Hollywood High cherished the international reputation conferred upon it by the chosen few, but they were expected to keep their self-importance within bounds.

Besides, acting was far from being the only route to prestige on campus. School productions were well attended, but so were football games, and athletic stardom was still considered to be the ultimate form of celebrity. And by the mid-Thirties, there were enough different sports on the roster to keep the school well supplied with all manner of athletic heroes. In 1936 softball was made a minor school sport, and a "Goof" football team was organized for those not good enough for the varsity but too big for the B (or junior varsity) team. The school also had its science buffs, musicians, debaters, and scholars, all too preoccupied with their own respective interests to pay much attention to the latest screen gossip. Among certain groups of students, winning a local science fair was just as valid a form of celebrity as being chosen for a small part in a motion picture.

In many other respects as well, Hollywood High was a relentlessly normal American high school. Rowdyism was still a popular indulgence, and in 1936 the punishment for smoking on campus was upped to expulsion. (Until then it had been ten detention periods.) Students at Hollywood High were just as anxious about grades as their peers around the country—the school's academic requirements had remained stringent—and cheating on exams had become so common by then that the school paper published an editorial describing (and of course

decrying) the ten most popular methods. The description makes clear that the students of Hollywood High
were fluent in the international language of cheating—
writing notes on handkerchiefs, printing dates on hands
and fingernails, using sign language to convey the answers for true/false questions (two fingers for true, one
for false), and passing around erasers inscribed with
notes. Chances are the paper's detailed exposé did more
to educate those unaware of the nuances of cheating than
to dissuade its practitioners.

Assemblies were still mandatory several times a week
and still considered less than enthralling by a number of
the students, though the mid-Thirties saw programs featuring talents as varied as organist E. Power Biggs, the world's
fastest typist, a meat cutter, a chalk artist, a crew of Swiss
yodelers, and a group of players who presented a drama-
tization of the evils of narcotics entitled *The Judge and the
Dope Peddler*. Perhaps the most exciting assembly of the era
occurred on a Tuesday morning in October 1937. "TELE-
VISION DISPLAY TO BE IN ASSEMBLY," the school paper proclaimed a full week before the event, alerting the
student body to "wear your best bib and tucker to school
Tuesday. Remember to wash behind your ears and comb
your hair. Get out of bed on the right side that morning
and come to school with your most charming expression.
On that day you'll stand a very good chance to see yourself
as others see you—in short, you might be 'televisioned'!"
Apathetic as many of the students may have been toward
assemblies, the hands shot up throughout the auditorium
when Professor Walter Everman asked for volunteers, and
a hush descended over the room when he said, "Television
will be an everyday reality in the private homes of America
by 1939 and probably sooner."

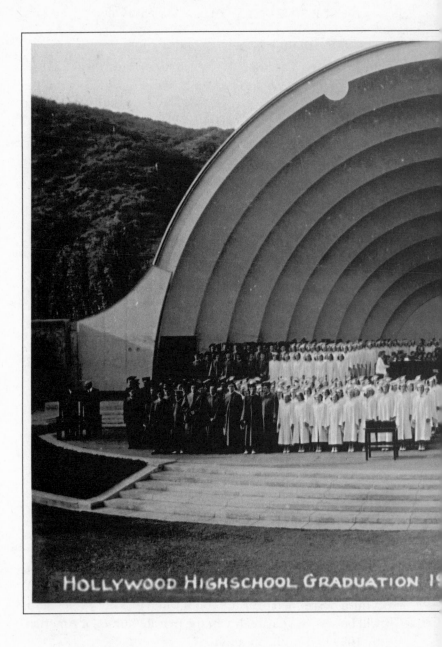
HOLLYWOOD HIGHSCHOOL GRADUATION 19

OLLYWOOD BOWL HOLLYWOOD, CAL. 394

1939.

1.

There is one thing I'm going to see to as far as it is in my power, and that is that every boy and girl in Hollywood High School is going to know all the words to "America," "The Star-Spangled Banner," and "The Loyalty Song."
—From an assembly speech given by
Principal Louis Foley, November 1941

Though the conflict in Europe had received some attention in the pages of *The Hollywood High School News* in the late Thirties—the paper reprinted a series of impassioned letters from an alumna who had been aboard a torpedoed British liner, and one 1939 debate topic concerned the pros and cons of an American alliance with Great Britain—by most accounts, the majority of Hollywood High's student body was as indifferent to the subject as an earlier generation had been to World War I—before it became their war. To many students, Adolf Hitler was just a funny little man who bore a striking resemblance to Charlie Chaplin.

By mid-1940, however, the prospect of American involvement in the war began to seem real. Hollywood High's mobilization, if it can be called that, was largely psychological, but there were practical aspects to it as well. The school's award-winning ROTC battalion, one of the highest-rated in the nation, began drilling with a new purpose, "realizing," in the words of *The Poinsettia*, "that it might be necessary at any time to protect our great democracy from invasion." (That same *Poinsettia* had as its theme "The Principles of Democracy.") The school band was given new, more military-looking uniforms (featuring Pershing caps), and a three-week course in national defense stressing "civilian defense, the geography of defense and the place of women in defense" was made a graduation requirement for all seniors. Principal Louis Foley, appalled by the ignorance of the students in the area of patriotic lyrics, promised severe retribution to any senior who failed to memorize the words to "America," "The Star-Spangled Banner," and "The Loyalty Song." Even the school newspaper's haughty fashion arbiter (an anonymous student who wrote under the pen name "Miss Hollywood") pitched in, proclaiming the stylishness of "patriotic pins and tiny American flags . . . on sweaters, blouses and jackets." (Until then, Miss Hollywood had limited her advisories to Dorothy Lamour–inspired sarongs, simplicity of dress, and the latest rage in do-it-yourself jewelry: dog biscuits strung into a necklace.)

Editorials stressing enlistment in the Army began appearing in 1940, resolutions regarding the pros and cons of the military draft dominated the debate club, and early the following year one of the school's most beloved football coaches, Boris Pash, whose teams were familiarly known as "The Pashmen," stunned the student body by announcing his departure from school to become a captain in the U.S. Army. That year's commemoration of Armistice Day took on a particularly ominous tone. "On this, the 23rd Armistice Day, with war clouds engulfing many of the nations of the world and hanging threateningly and darkly over our own beloved democracy, it is fitting that we resolve to give our full measure of devotion and sacrifice to our country in her preparations to meet the terrors and hardships that seem to lie ahead," read the school paper's editorial.

Meanwhile, war clouds or no, spaghetti was voted the most popular food served in the cafeteria (with lemon pie running a close second), pigtails were taking the campus by storm, the senior prom had a nautical theme, and "What Motion Pictures Mean to Me" was the subject of the Chamber of Commerce's annual essay contest. The coming war may have been on everyone's mind by then, but there was still plenty of room for the usual diversions.

It was in the midst of this peculiar calm-before-the-storm atmosphere that Jason Robards, Jr., received his diploma from Hollywood High in the summer of 1940.

2.

In the feature race, Jason Robards, Redshirt mile
ace, won the event in 4:47:4, but was disqualified.

—From the sports page of
*The Hollywood High School
News*, May 1939.

Though his father had
been a star of stage and screen in the Twenties, young
Jason Robards, Jr., was not disposed toward an acting
career, at least not during his tenure at Hollywood High.
By the time he was of high school age, his father's acting
career had fallen on lean days and the family was forced
to move to a smaller, less flashy house in the Hollywood
foothills, where young Robards spent most of his youthful days playing sports in a nearby sandlot. As a result,
he was not a "Hollywood Brat" in the conventional sense
(though he attended the same junior high school as Judy
Garland), and his father's hardships may even have
turned him off to the profession. When he entered Hollywood High in the late Thirties, he was intent on becoming a journalist, though by graduation he would list
"radio announcer" as his chosen vocation. (The idea of
becoming a professional athlete also appealed to him for
a while.) Hollywood High's drama department failed to
inspire him. Though he took dramatics as part of an English course, he was put off by the teacher, who, as Robards recalled, "spent a lot of time imitating George

Ace miler Jason Robards (right) winning a race against rival University High, 1939.

Jason Robards's yearbook picture, or one of them anyway. For some reason, he appears in two yearbooks.

Arliss and getting us to memorize Shakespeare, which almost killed Shakespeare for me. Whenever I got up to speak, I shook all over. I practically flunked dramatics, and the only reason they passed me was that they needed me for the track team. I was the best miler they had."

It was in athletics that Robards made a name for himself at Hollywood High. All told, he participated in football, baseball, and basketball at various times, but his greatest success was in track. His junior year, he was the school's best mile runner, and by his senior year he was captain of the cross-country team. He was known as Hollywood High's "ace distance man," and from all accounts, he was a natural. "Jason Robards placed third in the Western League," crooned the sports page of the school paper in 1938, "which is very good for a boy who had never run the mile before this season." At the time, the school record for the mile, set in 1935, was four minutes twenty-eight seconds. Robards broke it easily and set a new record of four minutes twenty-one seconds. He won a varsity letter in 1939 and was offered a number of track scholarships.

By his junior year he was something of a school sports celebrity. His name appeared several times in the "Pert Personals" column of the school paper (one such item described his surprise at finding six lemons in his lunch box one afternoon, though it's unknown who put them there or what happened to his lunch), and he was asked to contribute a quote about the school for the 1939 yearbook. "My three years at Hollywood High have been the happiest of my life," young Jason Robards wrote. "The fine direction of the principal and vice-principal have made possible this happy stay. I dread parting from the campus which has grown to be a place of lasting beauty."

A year later, Robards graduated, listing Spanish as his best subject and "Iowa" as his chosen college. The war, however, would interrupt his plans. This item appeared in a 1943 issue of the school newspaper, which by that time had begun to print a regular column called "News of Boys from the Front": "Jason Robards, S'40, is a radioman third class in the Navy and is waiting in San Francisco for orders for overseas duty. He witnessed the bombing of Pearl Harbor and has been in 13 major sea engagements." Robards would not become a well-known screen star until the late Fifties, but by that time he had already distinguished himself as an actor on the legitimate stage. Years later, Jason Robards would be honored by Hollywood High's Alumni Association with the school's coveted "Achieve the Honorable Award."

3.

Teacher: "What was the Age of Pericles?"
Student: "I'm not sure, but I think it was about forty."

—Conversation overheard in
history class

In the morning of December 8, 1941, Franklin Delano Roosevelt's "War Message to Congress" blasted from every loudspeaker of Hollywood High's public address system. Few alumni will ever forget that day. From the gym locker room to the auditorium to biology class, everyone on campus heard the dire news.

Curiously, no mention of Pearl Harbor appears in the school newspaper from December 1941 through the end of the year. It was as if nothing at all had happened. Instead of running banner headlines decrying the Japanese surprise attack, the December 10, 1941, issue of *The Hollywood High School News* opted for "Senior Glee Clubs to Sing Yule Songs" as its major news story, and that week's editorial did not rage against the dastardly deed in the Pacific, but berated students for careless driving. Three subsequent editions of the paper continued to make Pearl Harbor conspicuous by its absence from the headlines—or anywhere else. Judging from the newspaper alone, the major events of interest to the students that month were the Christmas program put on by the

Orchesis Club, the singing of Christmas carols in a student assembly, and Principal Foley's veto of a proposed fifth-period cleanup hour. Of course it is not the function of a school newspaper to report news already well covered by the professional press, but one might have expected at least some mention of Pearl Harbor in the paper's overcrowded pages.

Whatever the case, it would not be long before the unpleasant reality of the situation dominated not only the newspaper's headlines, but the school's proceedings as well. By the start of the New Year, the campus was seriously gearing up for war, a mobilization initially motivated by very immediate fears. After all, the Japanese had already bombed nearby Hawaii; maybe Los Angeles would endure the next surprise attack. These fears, though often mocked today as overreaction, were not unfounded. Three days after Pearl Harbor, local antiaircraft guns blasted away at a squadron of unidentified planes flying toward Los Angeles. Shrapnel from the big guns pelted roofs all over Hollywood, and shock waves could be felt from MGM to Paramount. Presumed to be Japanese, the planes quickly disappeared over the Pacific, leaving nothing but a frightened population in their wake. (Satirists would later dub the encounter "The Battle for Hollywood," and it would become the subject of Steven Spielberg's film *1941*.) But city officials were not amused and quickly responded by imposing a blackout, ordering citizens to switch off their lights by six o'clock every night. Those who didn't comply would fall prey to angry mobs who roamed the streets, smashing storefront windows and putting out the lights themselves. Three months later, on February 24, 1942, another attack occurred when a Japanese submarine shelled an oil field just north of Santa Barbara. Though the sub fired sixteen shells, there were no casualties and only one derrick suffered damage. "Their marksmanship was rotten," claimed an eyewitness quoted in the pages of *The Los Angeles Times*.

Insulated as it may have been from outside events, Hollywood High was hardly immune from the hysteria that swept the city. "In the event of an air raid," the school paper announced, "Hollywood High will become the community first aid center for this district." Under the direction of Principal Foley, who was duly appointed "emergency shelter administrator," and local civilian defense officials, enough food and first aid equipment were collected to keep students sheltered from an air raid for ten days. Desks, tables, and benches would serve as dining facilities in the event of an attack, and all members of the faculty were required to take a Red Cross training course.

School fire squads were appointed and trained for emergency situations. "In case of incendiary bombs falling on the roof," the school paper assured its readers, "the fire squads have assumed the responsibility to get on the roof and put out the bombs." As for the other students—in the event of an air raid, they were instructed to lie facedown, cover their ears with the palms of their hands, and keep their mouths open to reduce the effects of the concussion. ("We spent a lot of time crouching under our desks," says one wartime student.) A separate list of instructions was posted on how students could best survive a gas attack. (Campus wits suggested abstaining from cafeteria food for two days.)

The school curriculum was also altered as a result of the national emergency. Instead of social studies, seniors were required to take a new version of the course called "National Defense," in which, among other activities, the drawing of war maps was part of the instruction. Victory gardens were grown in biology, war posters were designed in art class, and the Hollywood High night school offered courses in civilian defense techniques. Extracurricular activities now included selling war bonds ($21,230 worth were purchased by students as early as February 1942) and—putting a traditional activity to new uses—holding benefit dances with themes like "The National Defense Dance" to raise money for the war effort. Miss Hollywood's column informed students that the "V for Victory proudly displayed on your socks, sweaters, gloves, and vanity cases is becoming an accessory 'must.'" The class of 1942 even went so far as to give up class sweaters to save money.

No school activity was immune from the economic strictures and safety precautions imposed by the school board that year, not even the annual spring play. Since all evening gatherings of students were now prohibited due to the blackout, *Robin Hood* would be presented in two parts at two daytime assemblies, rather than at night, as was the usual procedure. Moreover, the board's new set of wartime economic restrictions frowned upon spending money on such frivolous items as scenery, backdrops, and costumes when that money could better be used to buy uniforms and ammunition for the boys at the front. As a result, *Robin Hood* would be performed on a bare stage, with no props, costumes, or scenery. In fact, there would not be much of anything. "There will be very little, if any, dialogue, or stage business," the school paper explained. "The audience will be called upon to use its imagination to supply these. This will be a unique and original way of presenting the spring opera." Fortunately, these restrictions were soon loosened, and the school's productions, though less extravagant than before, were restored to at least a fair semblance of their traditional format.

At the outset of the war, only twenty-year-olds were being drafted. "Everybody thought it would be over within a year," recounts a member of 1942's senior class. "If you were seventeen years old, you just figured it wasn't your war." Nevertheless, a considerable number of students, mostly seniors, enlisted in the armed forces. To do this, they did not have to go far—the district recruitment office was set up in the lobby of Hollywood High's auditorium. Though the school heartily endorsed enlistment, there was a certain degree of dismay at how the sudden paucity of males was taking its toll on the school's athletics teams. By February 1942, for example, three celebrated members of Hollywood High's track team had departed, two for the Marines, one for the Navy. "With these three track stars gone," the school paper lamented, "Hollywood will have pretty rough competition in the coming track meets." As it turned out, of course, competition was no rougher than usual, for every high school team in the city was losing its best athletes to the war.

Rationing and conservation soon cramped the students' style even more. Gasoline was needed to fuel fighter planes and tanks; rubber, which was in short supply at the time, was necessary for military tires. To bring this point home to the students who regularly drove to school, a 1942 edition of *The Hollywood High School News* posed the editorial question, "Japs or Jalopies?" "Is a broken-down jalopy really of more value than the rights of liberty and democracy?" the paper asked rhetorically. "Oil up your knee joints and start walking!"

I only ask that when I die
You'll carry me back to Hollywood High.
Lay my algebra on my chest,
And tell Mr. Overfield I did my best.
Lay my English by my side
And tell Miss Grundy I'm glad I died.
Lay my Latin at my head,
And tell Mrs. Abbot that's why I'm dead.
          —From *The Hollywood High School News*, 1942

ack in 1925, when the prospects for the lasting world peace seemed somewhat more promising, a student competition called "The League of Nations Contest" was set up in the Los Angeles school district. High school students wishing to enter the competition were required to take an examination in essay form, focused on the theme of organizing the world for peace. The winner received a free, all-expenses-paid trip to Europe.

The League of Nations Contest soon became an annual tradition, and a fair number of Hollywood High students entered each year. In 1940, against the background of Hitler's incursions into Poland and Czechoslovakia, the contest's sponsors stubbornly announced that the competition would be "conducted this year as in other years regardless of world conditions." The prize, believe it or not, was still a free trip to Europe.

Traditions die hard, and the League of Nations Contest, absurd as it may have become, continued throughout the war. In 1942, with the entire world in flames, the "problems of organizing the world for peace" was still the competition's theme. By then, however, even the contest's sponsors had to admit that Europe no longer provided the best example of peace in action, and was a dangerous place to vacation besides. As a concession to reality, the prize was altered. A free, all-expense-paid trip to South America was substituted that year.

By 1943, in light of the fact that organizing the world for peace seemed utterly hopeless for the time being, the competition finally changed its theme. Entrants were now asked to consider the problems of organizing the world for *postwar* peace.

5.

As for romance—one boy's comment on Mickey Rooney films says a lot: "Mickey acts like a junior high school big shot. We don't make as much fuss about kissing as he does. If we want to kiss a girl, we kiss her and that's that."

—From a 1941 *Look* magazine
piece on Hollywood High

The war was one thing, but it was not the only thing, at least not at Hollywood High. By the early Forties, Lana Turner had become a full-fledged star, and her alma mater basked in more than just a glimmer of the spotlight. Though Lana's tenure at the school had been fleeting, studio publicists made the most of it, and before long every fan magazine in America carried the inspirational saga of how young Judy Turner cut a typing class one afternoon and dashed across the street to become a star. Hollywood High was now the most famous school in America, a jumping-off point for aspiring stars, the starting gate in the race for screen celebrity. Publicists and fan magazines referred to it regularly as "The Star Hatchery" or "The Starlet Factory," and in 1941 *Look* magazine ran a three-page pictorial on the school in which it was observed that "the girls are perhaps more style-conscious than they would be in other cities and that may account for the large number who seem exceptionally attractive." The students themselves may have been blasé about all the fanfare, but more than a few local stage mothers with stagestruck daughters were inspired enough to actually move across town to the Hollywood school district to give their babies a chance to duplicate Lana's serendipitous "discovery." One can only wonder how many hopeful young Hollywood High coeds have since lingered interminably (not to mention erroneously) over milk shakes at Schwab's in expectation of that fateful tap on the shoulder.

Though no one would ever again be discovered in quite the same way as Lana, Hollywood High still managed to produce a prodigious number of "discoveries" during the war years. Soap opera star Lois (*Edge of Night*) Kibbee, who graduated in 1940, made the short march from the school auditorium to the studio lot after playing the Duchess of Mudland in 1939's school production of *Ermine*. Peggie Castle, a second-feature leading lady during the Fifties and costar of the TV series *Lawman,* was a member of the class of 1943, as was television travel host Bill Burrud. Burrud distinguished himself on campus during those turbulent war years as a student Red Cross assistant assigned to the second floor of the Administration building.

The class of 1942 produced two notable graduates: Academy Award–winning actress Gloria Grahame and the Carter Administration's assistant secretary of state, Warren Christopher, both of whom were heavily involved in the school's debating society. Grahame, whose real name was Gloria Hallward, was born in Los Angeles in 1925, the daughter of English stage actress Jean Grahame. Known primarily for playing blond bombshell roles in the movies, Gloria was once described by Cecil B. DeMille as having "the eyes of a sorceress and the manner of a schoolgirl." At Hollywood High, she seems to have posed another sort of contradiction to her schoolmates, for, though she was said to be "very shy," she participated in many school productions and managed to win two West Coast Forensic League Championships. Movie contracts and drama school scholarships were offered to her throughout her high school career, but Gloria rejected them, claiming that she was waiting for the right offer.

The right offer came just a month prior to her graduation in the winter of 1942. One hundred thirty-five Hollywood High students had tried out for the meager eleven parts in the drama department's upcoming production of *Ever Since Eve,* a popular light comedy about an overzealous young lady named Susan Blake who takes over a small local newspaper edited by two of her friends and attempts to save it from financial ruin. "I think it has lots of possibilities, the way she screws everything up and gets everyone into trouble," young Gloria Hallward gushed to the school newspaper after getting the lead part. "I'm just thrilled to death!"

In the best tradition of the clichéd Hollywood success story, stage producer Howard Lang happened to be in the audience on opening night and was captivated enough by Gloria's performance to offer her a job as understudy in his new show, *Good Night Ladies.* She completed her studies by mail and went on to star in the Chicago opening of the production. Two years later she made her film debut in *Blonde Fever*, and by 1952—after appearing in such classics as *It's a Wonderful Life* and

Crossfire—she won an Academy Award for her performance in *The Bad and the Beautiful*.

Warren Christopher's high school career, like Gloria
Grahame's, would prove to be an accurate indicator of
future career moves. When thirteen-year-old Warren enrolled in the class of 1942, his ambition was to become
a lawyer, and he soon established himself as one of the
school's finest speakers. As a novice debater in 1940, he
cut his teeth on a number of popular prewar issues such
as the pros and cons of the military draft. In 1941 he
successfully argued the negative side of such topics as
"Resolved: That the power of the federal government
should be increased." During his senior year he was
elected vice-president of the service club and placed first
in a citywide high school debate championship, a competition in which Christopher's debating colleague, Gloria Hallward (whom he does not remember), would have
participated had she not left school a few weeks earlier
to pursue her acting career.

"In those days," says Christopher, "debating had a
higher standing at Hollywood High than at most other
schools, mainly because of Hollywood High's emphasis
on drama and public speaking. The debate coach, Nor-
man McLeod, was very inspiring to his students. He in-
sured that we were always very well prepared. I remember
being nervous before each debate and for the first two
or three minutes of each debate, but once I got going, I
was more relaxed." If it hadn't been for debating, Warren Christopher might never have been able to afford to
go to college—his speaking ability was rewarded by a
scholarship to Redlands College in 1942.

Though an able student and an active one, young

Hollywood High's 1942 production of *Ever Since Eve* starred an attractive senior named Gloria Grahame (far left).

Warren Christopher did not go out for sports at Hollywood High. ("The school did not lose a great champion athlete," he confesses.) Like many youngsters of the Depression era, he was compelled to work after school. "I always had a job," he recalls. "For a time I was a messenger and copyboy for *The Hollywood Citizen News*. I'd usually leave school at two or three o'clock in the afternoon and work until eight. Naturally, this put some limitation on my involvement in school activities and precluded me from participating in sports." When the war came, young Warren Christopher came up with an ingenious way of keeping his classmates informed. "I organized a type of radio news show that came on during the noon hour," he recalls. "We'd give the war news over loudspeakers to all the students eating lunch."

In 1942, as part of the war effort, an organization called the Student Speakers Bureau was formed, and Christopher became one of its most active members. The purpose of the SSB was to inform schools and other city organizations such as the Kiwanis and Lions Clubs on subjects of "vital interest in civilian defense." Students with public-speaking ability were asked to join the club and give rousing speeches on such subjects as "Patriotism," "Thrift," and "Defense Bonds." The future assistant secretary of state spoke to members of the Kiwanis and the Lions Clubs and made a tour of Hollywood High homerooms. According to *The Hollywood High School News*, his speech was entitled "Waste Paper."

6.

POSTCARDS FROM MANZANAR

Hollywood High's primarily white, middle-class student body had always been peppered with a random assortment of minorities. Though blacks and Latinos were seldom seen on campus prior to the Fifties, Asians were present in relatively high numbers from the school's first years. Students of Chinese and Japanese descent had, as a general rule, excelled at the school throughout its history, and many were honored with the school's highest achievement awards. (One Japanese-American student, the class of 1926's John Aiso, had been one of Hollywood High's most outstanding scholars and went on to become an aide to General MacArthur and later a Superior Court judge.) By the late Thirties, there were enough Japanese-American kids at the school to provide a sizable membership roster for the newly formed Japanese club.

Then came the bombing of Pearl Harbor and the subsequent war hysteria. Los Angeles's Little Tokyo became an overnight ghost town. Japanese-Americans who worked for the studios were told not to return to work until the government had determined their status. (Most of them were never rehired.) At Hollywood High, the Japanese club was unceremoniously disbanded, and the faces of the school's Japanese-American students suddenly disappeared from the pages of *The Poinsettia* from 1943 all the way through 1945.

The first contingent of Japanese-Americans to be sent to the Manzanar "relocation camp" departed in March 1942. Adalene Maki, a graduate of the class of 1944, remembers the event: "The Japanese-American students were generally thought of on campus as the smart ones, the brains. One of them was my best friend. I'll never forget the day she came in crying and said she had to leave for a while. We used to get letters from her about how barren and cold it was in the camps."

"It was a very sad time," says Warren Christopher, a senior when the relocations began. "I thought it was just terrible. I wasn't mature enough to criticize the policy, but I was very saddened by it."

If there was any evidence of student outcry against the relocation program, the school paper did not publicize it. In fact, *The Hollywood High School News* gave no mention of the issue until June 10, 1942, by which time many of the Japanese-American students had already been shipped off. The article that did appear on that date is a fairly transparent mixture of adolescent naiveté and wartime propaganda. The editors euphemistically asserted that the missing students had gone to "reception centers in Pomona, Santa Anita and Manzanar," where "every comfort is being shown the Japanese people." The thrust of the article had to do with letters the interned Japanese students had written to their teachers at Hollywood High regarding their new accommodations.

"This camp life is really quite boring," one student wrote. "There's nothing to do here and all we do is eat and sleep."

"The government is taking good care of us," another stated. "For our baseball games we have a good cheering section."

And another reported, "In the evening we have a band concert and community singing; we also have dances every Wednesday and Saturday night."

Sadly, the editors of the school paper, products of their time caught up in the patriotic fervor of the day, concluded with smugly adolescent illogic: "If the American people now interned in Japan are being so considerately treated, their friends and relatives in the U.S. should have little cause for worry."

7.

BUY STAMPS TO BLACK OUT DER FUEHRER!
—Slogan for Hollywood High's
defense stamp drive

Not long before gradua-
tion day, 1942, Hollywood High had its first genuine war
hero. Alumnus Ted Lawson, a lieutenant in the Air Force
and member of the class of 1935, had piloted one of the
planes in the famous Doolittle bombing raid over Tokyo.
"HOLLYWOOD HIGH SENDS GREETINGS TO HI-
ROHITO," rang the proud headline in *The Hollywood
High School News*. Lawson, it was noted, had been an excellent scholar and swimmer during his tenure on campus. He would go on to coauthor the bestselling book
Thirty Seconds Over Tokyo.

But Lawson was only one of thousands of Hollywoodians who joined the armed services during World
War II. Between 1942 and 1945, seventy-five percent of
all Hollywood families had at least one member in uniform, some thirty thousand men in all. Within a month
of the so-called Battle for Hollywood, over one thousand
film industry workers—stars, technicians, directors, and
writers—had enlisted, and by the end of the year their
number had swelled sevenfold. Clark Gable joined the

Army; Tyrone Power signed up with the Marines; and Henry Fonda enlisted in the Navy.

But Hollywood was of even greater value to the war effort for its proven fund-raising capabilities. Not long after Pearl Harbor, an outfit called the Hollywood Victory Committee was established to send stars on nation-wide fund-raising tours. By the end of the war, the committee had raised millions. Bob Hope, Bing Crosby, Al Jolson, and Eddie Cantor were Hollywood's star bond salesmen. Ginger Rogers sold her dancing shoes for $10,000 worth of war bonds, and Veronica Lake auctioned off a lock of her hair for $185,000. Marlene Dietrich, Betty Grable, Dorothy Lamour, and Hollywood High's own Lana Turner boosted morale by posing for barrack pinups. Benefit programs were also high on Hollywood's wartime agenda. In April 1943, the Hollywood Bowl was temporarily redecorated (by MGM's art director, Cedric Gibbons) for a David O. Selznick–produced extravaganza to raise funds for the United China Relief Fund. Spencer Tracy and seaman Henry Fonda were among the featured speakers, and some twenty major female stars took part in a lavish pageant dedicated to the guest of honor, Madame Chiang Kai-shek.

In many ways, the war effort enlivened the community, replacing the grinding doldrums of the Depression with a new spirit of single purpose. Despite rationing and blackouts, Hollywood became a bustling center of activity. The film industry, which had just managed to survive the Thirties, was showing renewed strength with a healthy $735 million profit in 1940. (By 1945 the figure would double.) Hollywood Boulevard, which had become a hangout for hobos and oddballs during the Depression years, took on a festival atmosphere during the war. Nearby, on Sunset and Cahuenga, was the legendary Hollywood Canteen, founded in 1942 by Bette Davis and John Garfield. Here, free of charge, GIs on leave from the Pacific could jitterbug the night away with the likes of Joan Crawford, Marlene Dietrich, Betty Grable, and Hedy Lamarr. Sometimes Crawford would take groups of soldiers to her Brentwood home for dinner. And as part of a regularly scheduled Canteen magic show, Orson Welles would saw Rita Hayworth in half every night.

Life at Hollywood High, however, was somewhat less enthralling, for the war had taken a toll on practically every traditional recreation of student life. "School dances were dreadful during the war," recounts Adalene Maki. "Hardly anybody went, and a lot of them were called off because it was too dangerous to let the kids out at night. It wasn't easy getting dates either, unless you went to the USO. Some girls did, but most of us were too shy." Due to the national emergency, the football team was prohibited from traveling to and from other schools, and practice games were eliminated. For most students, driving to school was now taboo—those who lived near bus stops were instructed to leave their jalopies at home; others were required to drive at least four other students to school in order to qualify for extra gas rations. Because of the meat shortage, hamburgers and hot dogs were no longer available at the campus lunch stand—chiliburgers, made out of beans, cheese, and chili, were sold instead. The yearbook, once a thick hardbound volume, was reduced to a fifteen-page softcover pamphlet for four consecutive years due to paper rationing.

And, much to the chagrin of the school's glamorous coeds, the boys were leaving in ever greater numbers. To provide the nation with as many new recruits as possible, Hollywood High had established a wartime program of accelerated study in January 1943. The purpose, of course, was to graduate students earlier so that they would then be eligible for participation in the war effort, either at home or abroad. Teaching was intensified, courses were condensed, credit for work experience was granted, and homework and physical fitness were emphasized. Students in the program could now get their diplomas at the age of sixteen. If you wanted a date with a boy from Hollywood High, you had to hurry.

The sudden dearth of handsome young men on campus changed a lot of things, not the least of which were the proprieties of dating. As the "Good Manners" booklet did not cover the nuances of wartime dating etiquette, Miss Hollywood took it upon herself to instruct the school's coeds on the dos and don'ts. "Men are scarce, gals," she observed in one column, "but that's no excuse for two of you effecting a share-the-man plan and making him walk between you!" Though that form of thrift was not encouraged, other kinds were. "Don't forget when you're dating a man in uniform," Miss Hollywood counseled her glamorous readers, "his pocketbook is only so big and capable of only a certain amount of spending." According to the school's arbiter of style and manners—and national security—it was permissible to "wink at him when he's marching in formation," but a no-no to ask him "any embarrassing questions that would compel him to say it's a military secret." Girls were further advised "never to ask him to carry packages or an umbrella. He'll do it of course, but it's considered unmilitary and is apt to get him into difficulties particularly when he has to salute an officer."

Of course, Hollywood High joined the rest of the community and did its part to raise funds. After all, since dances were a bust and dates were hard to come by, there was plenty of time for patriotic duty. Some students sold bonds and defense stamps, but others participated in more creative enterprises. One of these was a student-organized costume jewelry drive. Cheap trinkets and baubles were fashioned by the school's coeds and sent to GI's stationed in the South Pacific, the idea being that the soldiers could use the trinkets to barter with island natives for information regarding the whereabouts of the enemy. The drive's poetic slogan was, "Give a Clip to Nab a Nip."

8.

I wanted to play football for Hollywood High, but since I didn't show up for too many classes, I got kicked out.

—James Garner

During the next few years, Hollywood High continued to matriculate a steady succession of students bound for big-screen stardom, only this time there was a difference—the majority were boys. Until then, the school's glamorous coeds had dominated the classroom-to-studio-lot migration, but with so many handsome young men fighting overseas, the studios were hungry for fresh young male faces. Hollywood's steady production of war movies in particular required men out of uniform to play men *in* uniform, and though the usual crop of starlets still emerged from the campus between 1943 and 1946, the girls were seriously outnumbered by the boys.

One of the first of these was Richard Jaeckel, who got his start playing GIs in such films as *Guadalcanal Diary* and *Sands of Iwo Jima*. A member of the class of 1943, Jaeckel barely had time to frame his diploma before he was discovered by the studios. He had dabbled in dramatics at Hollywood High, but never gave much thought to becoming an actor. Like fellow alumnus Jason Robards, young Richard Jaeckel, known on campus as Jack, preferred athletics. He swam the hundred-yard breast-stroke on Hollywood High's swimming team in 1942 (one of the team's only undefeated seasons), and played football under difficult wartime conditions (no helmets, torn jerseys, and restricted practice games). His peers remember him primarily as "an all-around athlete."

A month or so after graduation, Jaeckel got a job as a messenger for 20th Century-Fox, his ambition being to work his way up to a production job, maybe even directing. As it happened, the studio was in the midst of casting for an upcoming war feature, the memorable *Guadalcanal Diary*. Jaeckel, a husky, attractive teenager who had spent time building his physique, was spotted by a producer and talked into taking a screen test. Only three months out of Hollywood High, the seventeen-year-old youngster had copped a significant film role. After a succession of war movies, he would go on to star in a number of prestigious films during the Fifties, Sixties, and Seventies. Today he's a regular on the TV series *Spenser: For Hire*.

Word of mouth led to Richard Long's chance discovery a year later. Long had moved to Hollywood from Evanston, Illinois, in 1943, and enrolled as a sophomore at Hollywood High. He joined the glee club and often sang bass in the school's annual spring operettas. During his senior year he got the male lead in Hollywood High's spring play, *Louisiana Susie*.

While young Dick Long was rehearsing his part for the school production, Universal-International Pictures was searching high and low for a young man to play Claudette Colbert's son in an upcoming feature called *Tomorrow Is Forever*. Screen tests had been made in Hollywood and New York, but the role was still unfilled. One morning in March 1945, U-I's casting director, Jack Murton, happened to be driving a couple of neighborhood kids to Hollywood High as part of the local wartime share-a-ride plan. Along the way, he inquired about the school's annual spring production and was told it was in rehearsal. He then asked about the cast, specifically as to whether there were any outstanding young male performers. Richard Long's name was mentioned. Murton contacted the young actor, a screen test was arranged, and seventeen-year-old Richard Long got not only the part but a long-term studio contract as well. "Dick made no effort to seek a screen career," *The Hollywood Citizen-News* reported less than a week later, "It sought him." Long, who died in 1974, made numerous movies after *Tomorrow Is Forever*, but he is best known today for his regular appearances in long-running television series like *77 Sunset Strip*, *Nanny and the Professor*, and *The Big Valley*. The last one featured another former Hollywood High student: Linda Evans.

While Richard Long was off rehearsing with Claudette Colbert, another Hollywood High student named Jim Bumgarner was about to get his first taste of show business. Bumgarner, who would eventually drop the first three letters of his last name, had moved from Oklahoma to Los Angeles as a teenager. Shortly after his freshman year, he quit high school to join the merchant marine, only to have the Germans surrender the moment he enlisted. On his return to Hollywood a year later, he worked with his father as a carpet layer for a few months, then decided to continue his education at Hollywood High. Academics was not the attraction. "I saw these good-

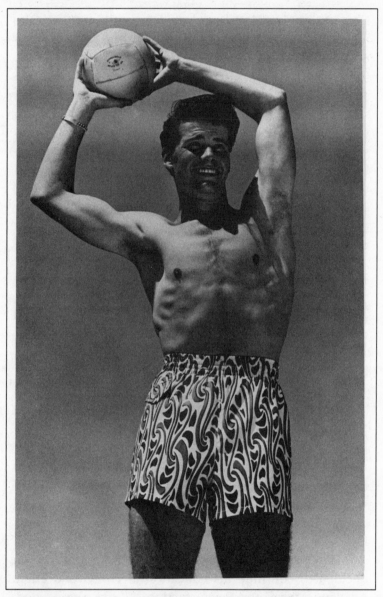

When representatives of Jantzen, Inc. came to campus looking for All-American boys to model their sportswear and swimwear, Hollywood High's varsity football coach recommended young James Garner. It was his first taste of show business.

looking girls who went to Hollywood High," he recalled, "and I said, 'That's for me.'"

By his own admission, Bumgarner was a less than average student, though he might have been a good one had he spent less time cutting classes. When not wandering the streets of Hollywood during school hours, he could usually be found at the beach or in a local pool parlor. Girls were attracted to him, but young Garner's classmates recollect that he was shy and did not date much. Aside from girls, the only thing that kept his interest in school was football. He was on the varsity team in 1945.

He was also the kind of kid who could never resist a dare, no matter how outlandish. "My buddies used to bet me I couldn't steal something," Garner remembers, "and I'd do it just to show 'em I could. My best was taking one of those four feet high peanut machines from Woolworth's. I just picked it up and walked out with aplomb, as if I was supposed to. After that, my friend Betty Jane Smith gave me the nickname Slick."

It was Garner's football coach, of all people, who introduced him to the world of show business. Early in 1945 the Jantzen sportswear company had sent a representative to Hollywood High looking for handsome All-American boys to model their swimwear in magazine ads. Slick Bumgarner's football coach recommended him along with nine others. At first young Jim wasn't interested. Modeling swimsuits was hardly his idea of how to spend an afternoon. But when the Jantzen rep mentioned that all models would be paid twenty dollars an hour, more than the Hollywood High principal earned, Jim Bumgarner signed up.

Garner never graduated from Hollywood High. He was eventually expelled for truancy and completed his education at a local trade school. The financial rewards of his first on-camera job may have made enough of an impression to motivate him toward an acting career, but James Garner would not achieve overnight success. Far from it. In spite of a succession of movie roles in the Fifties, he would not get his big break until 1957, when he was chosen to star in the TV series *Maverick*.

One of Jim Bumgarner's teammates on the Hollywood High football team was a young man named Stuart Whitman. The son of nomadic parents, Whitman had attended no less than twenty-six public schools all over the country before settling down at Hollywood High in 1943. Columnist Hedda Hopper summed up Whitman's pre–Hollywood High days in a 1958 column: "He admits he was a juvenile delinquent before he hit Hollywood High, where he received a solid part of his education."

Like Jason Robards, young Stuart Whitman had no interest in acting and was attracted instead to athletics, football in particular. He played right end on the B squad his sophomore year and was known as an excellent pass receiver. (He scored two touchdowns that year against Fairfax High.) In 1944, with his weight at 160, he made the varsity, playing end, and received his letter at the close of the season. By his junior year, he was a bona fide high school football hero and toyed with the idea of going professional after school, until a hip injury dashed his hopes. After a stint in the Army, Whitman turned to acting, first on the stage, then in a long succession of movies, beginning with the 1952 science fiction classic, *When Worlds Collide*.

A bona fide high-school football hero, Stuart Whitman played end on the varsity team and considered going professional.

9.

It's a great life running a school, hotel and dining room.

—Principal Louis Foley, 1944

Early in 1944 Hollywood High once again achieved national attention, only this time it had nothing to do with the movies.

With the war in the Pacific heating up and the famous Hollywood Canteen receiving national publicity, Hollywood had become host to thousands of GIs on weekend passes. Unfortunately, the beleaguered city did not have sufficient facilities to accommodate the ever-increasing numbers of soldiers wishing to spend their free time in the movie capital. The hotels were packed every weekend, and most private residences were not equipped to put up more than one or two men. Something had to be done.

The solution was obvious. Hollywood High had provided accommodations for soldiers on leave during World War I, so why not repeat the favor? After all, the school had an enormous new gym with enough floor space to accommodate hundreds of GIs. Moreover, the ventilation was excellent, the heating was adequate, and there were facilities for hot and cold showers. A member of the local Chamber of Commerce approached the

In 1944, Hollywood High once again achieved notoriety when it turned its gymnasium into a hospitality center for soldiers and sailors on weekend passes. Every Sunday morning, a bevy of blushing coeds served breakfast to the masses of hungry GIs.

school board with the idea and received immediate approval. Within a few days, the community sprang into action. The students managed to scare up $650 for the towel fund, the Hollywood chapter of the American Legion collected contributions for Sunday cleanups, David O. Selznick threw in $1,300, and the city's civic organizations provided funds for mattresses, dishes, blankets, and pillows. In January 1944 the "Hollywood High School Hotel and Restaurant" was open for business. "On opening night," the school paper reported, "Army and Navy guests were cheerfully served by Miss Heep's 6th period gym class."

It was a roaring success. As many as 900 soldiers could sleep comfortably on the gym floor (on New Year's Eve 1945, some 1,222 managed to fit), and every Sunday morning for the next two years, up to 1,500 of them were served a breakfast consisting of one orange, a bowl of hot cereal with milk and sugar, one fried egg, potatoes, toast, and coffee by an efficient crew of Hollywood High volunteers, most of them blushing teenage girls. *Life* magazine picked up on the story in April 1944, featuring a photo spread of Hollywood High's "pretty, smiling high school girls" dishing out chow to the bone-weary GIs.

One of those "pretty, smiling high school girls" was the class of 1946's Nina Blanchard, who signed up as a volunteer when the Hollywood High "Hotel" began in 1944 and worked tirelessly every Sunday morning until the makeshift accommodation closed down in 1946. She started as a silverware polisher her sophomore year, then worked at the directory desk, where her job included giving directions to the visiting GIs, seeing to it that their cards and letters were mailed, and, in her own words, "just talking to them for a while." Today Nina Blanchard runs one of the country's most prominent modeling agencies, but in those days, she was devoted to her work at the "Hotel." In fact, she distinguished herself among her covolunteers by being one of only two girls not to miss a single weekend during the facility's entire two-year life span. For this achievement, she was honored by her fellow students and featured on the front page of the school paper. "It makes me glow all over to hear compliments about our service work," she was quoted as saying in the article. "I only wish we could do more."

Nina Blanchard graduated with the winter class of 1946, by which time the Hollywood High "Hotel" was about to come to the end of its days. It had lasted for a full two years, but after V-J Day, the number of soldiers requiring bed and breakfast had decreased sharply, and on March 16, 1946, the mattresses were hauled out. Breakfasts continued for another three weeks, then ended on April 3. The volunteers, sad to see their soldier friends leaving for good, threw a farewell picnic at Griffith Park in their honor. All together, 92,597 GIs had spent the night at the Hollywood High gym.

10.

PARLEZ-VOUS FRANÇAIS?

Throughout World War II, the United States had been a haven for European refugees fortunate enough to manage escape from the conflict abroad. The East Coast had, of course, received most of this wartime immigration, but a smattering of refugees had made the journey west to California, and true to form, Hollywood High snagged a member of the show business contingent.

In 1941, German-born filmmaker Max Ophuls, then living in France, packed up his family and fled his adopted country for the sanctuary of America. To continue in his profession, he settled in Hollywood, and enrolled his teenage son, Marcel, at Hollywood High. Marcel Ophuls would go on in later years to follow in his father's footsteps, directing such internationally acclaimed films as *The Sorrow and the Pity*, but he would never forget his unusual tenure at an American high school.

The young Frenchman must have been something of an oddity at Hollywood High's hep all-American campus, where saddle shoes and bobby sox were the predominant styles in 1945. Wearing what must have been espadrilles, he elicited the notice of the school paper's "Pert Personals" column: "Marcel Ophuls," it read, "explained that his unusual sandals were 'left-overs from my trip to the south of France.'" Odd as he may have seemed, Ophuls must have fit in to a degree for, during his junior year, he ran for a seat on the student council, and his grades were high enough to land him on the honor roll. And, like many of his classmates, he got a small part in a Hollywood film. Director Frank Capra cast him in a wartime propaganda flick called *Prelude to War*. He played a Hitler youth.

Some years later, Marcel Ophuls remembered his years at Hollywood High as lonely and a bit strange. "I didn't catch on to the dating system, to American folkways like necking, rumble seats, football. My rationalization for my gawky loneliness was to consider myself very French, very sophisticated, blasé, a man of the world." No doubt the espadrilles helped.

11.

Bobby sox lose the shape of their wartime cuffs when washed. Try putting a rubber band around the tops while they're drying to keep them from stretching.

—Miss Hollywood, 1945

All told, 108 Hollywood High alumni fell in World War II, and many more were wounded or interned in enemy POW camps. The school paper's special wartime column, "News of Boys from the Front," continued through the first few postwar years, but shortly after V-J Day, students and members of the faculty who had enlisted in the armed services began returning to campus. One of these was former football coach Boris Pash, who had achieved some wartime fame as commander of a secret operation designed to round up German atomic materials and scientists.

Campus activity soon resumed its normal pace. The number of student clubs and organizations began to expand, though the defunct Japanese club did not reappear for years. *The Poinsettia*, which had shrunk to pamphlet size during the war to save money, returned to its old hardcover, multipaged format, and Japanese faces began to appear in its pages once again. Miss Hollywood abandoned her wartime advocacy of patriotic pins and victory gardens and turned to the new peacetime chic: "Fashions are turning away from the casual sportswear of the war years," she observed, "and the trend is now the well-groomed, ladylike look—hats and gloves are positive musts." Peacetime refinements aside, bobby sox, yo-yos, and moron jokes were all the rage.

Now that the wartime restriction on evening gatherings of students was no longer in effect, regular school dances were held again. Postwar proms were dressy affairs that generally included corsages, gowns, and dinner at a local restaurant. They were well attended, for, as the class of 1948's Rosita Smith put it, "If you didn't show up at the prom, you were considered a real loser. It was very important to be seen there. If you couldn't get a date, you'd have to import a cousin or something. The peer pressure was enormous." As for the other, less important dances, they fell prey to the usual old problems: The boys congregated in one corner ogling the girls, who were bunched in the other, while only the "steadies" tripped the light fantastic. The first sock hop took place in 1949.

The school newspaper forsook its wartime concerns for more traditional teen topics, becoming once again a lively forum for campus complaints. Mainly, these were of a social nature—the boys groused about the girls and vice versa. "We like to know whether we have a date and not be kept dangling," the boys grumbled. "Be ready on time. Only a boy knows how uncomfortable it can be trying to make conversation with your parents while you dilly dally getting ready. And please don't tell us about the cute guy you were out with last night." The girls fired back with complaints about how sloppily the boys dressed—T-shirts, Levi's, and army surplus leather jackets had become the standard uniform—and how they cracked gum, talked only about cars, and handed them phony lines. Guys who expected a kiss on the first date or asked permission to hold hands were also targets for attack.

Though no major stars graduated from Hollywood High between 1947 and 1949, the usual bevy of youthful starlets and extras still emerged from the campus. Actress Sheree North, whose real name was Dawn Bethel, attended the school for a time during the postwar years, but did not graduate. According to her 20th Century-Fox bio, she "left Hollywood High School at the principal's request after participating in a practice session with the football squad." By 1951 she had made her movie debut in *Eat My Dust,* soon to be followed by roles in *How to Be Very, Very Popular, The Best Things in Life Are Free,* and later, *Madigan, Charlie Varrick,* and *The Shootist.*

War might have made an indelible impression on the students of Hollywood High, but none had forgotten the school's special relationship with the film industry. In the spring of 1948, the student newspaper carried this headline: "Movie Stars to Take Hollywood High Teaching Positions Tomorrow." "Mr. Foley will vacate his office to Mr. Danny Kaye, who will serve as principal," the accompanying article proclaimed. "Boys sent down to the vice-principal's office will be dealt with by Jane Russell and girls by Ray Milland." Jimmy Durante would teach math, James Mason English, Rita Hayworth Spanish, Marlene Dietrich German, and Vera Vague would be debate coach. Lana Turner was slotted to handle senior problems, Betty Grable would lecture on psychology, and life science would be taught by Peter Lorre. Only at Hollywood High could such a fantasy have fooled a student audience for even a fraction of a second—but presumably it had its intended April Fool's Day effect at the high school of the stars.

PART FIVE

It's Only
Rock 'n' Roll

1950-1959

1.

People will soon get tired of staring at a plywood box every night.

> —A studio executive on
> the future of television

ack in 1939, when Hollywood High held an assembly demonstration of a new-fangled contraption called the "television," most of the students thought the invention was an interesting novelty, but few really believed that it would ever catch on. Unfortunately, most studio bosses, living up to their traditional lack of foresight, felt the same way. At first it appeared that this prediction was right, for television seemed to vanish from the scene almost as quickly as it had arrived. Of course, it never really disappeared—the development of video technology was simply delayed by the exigencies of the war effort. When the war ended, interest in television revived. It may have begun slowly (in 1946 only ten thousand American households had a TV set), but by 1950 the number of little "plywood boxes" in use had multiplied to just over three million. A year later the number would quadruple.

In its infancy, television programming in the Los Angeles area was nothing special. Local stations like KTTV broadcast a few popular shows like *Happy Hangs His Hat* and *Pantomime Quiz*, but these were little more than radio programs with pictures. Sid Caesar's *Your Show of Shows* was aired live in New York but was not available beyond the eastern market until 1952. Nevertheless, moviegoers were starting to stay home and watch TV. After all, it was entertainment, it was free, and you didn't need a baby-sitter.

The studios began to panic as early as 1948. That year, even though television was not especially widespread, box office receipts were down forty-five percent from wartime highs. But this was only the beginning. By 1950 movie attendance dropped to a new low of sixty million per week, the lowest figures since the worst year of the Depression. In 1951, with TV invading more and more American households, seven hundred movie theatres closed their doors. Some executives stubbornly held to the theory that TV was nothing more than a passing fad. Others predicted that Hollywood was finished forever. The numbers tended to support the pessimists, and a doomsday mood prevailed in Hollywood throughout the first years of the new decade. Instead of embracing TV as a new market for their products, the studios adamantly refused to cooperate and forbade their contract players from appearing in television shows.

While the studios were consumed with visions of impending doom brought on by TV, the American public was experiencing another sort of paranoia in the early days of the Fifties. During the initial postwar years, the United States had held a monopoly on the atomic bomb. But in the summer of 1949, while the students of Hollywood High and their counterparts across the nation were frolicking on the beach, the Soviet Union exploded its first atomic bomb. Suddenly the calm of postwar peace was shaken by the threat of atomic war.

In Los Angeles, the threat seemed especially immediate. For one thing, the city had spent the early years of World War II preparing for a Japanese surprise attack. Moreover, the area had recently become a center for the aircraft, oil, and aerospace industries and was thus considered a prime target in the event of atomic war. One of the nation's first fallout shelters was constructed in the backyard of a Los Angeles home in January 1951. And Hollywood covered it as only Hollywood could— with publicity flacks, studio photographers, and starlets in attendance at the ground-breaking ceremony. Local TV crews were also there.

Conscious that a new era was dawning, Hollywood High, ever at the forefront of any new trend, led off the Fifties with an assembly entitled "The Atom and You." Models of the atomic bomb, Geiger counters, and "radioactive materials" were put on display in the auditorium, and a lively question-and-answer period ensued. "This topic is extremely timely since, whether we like it or not, we are now living in an atomic age world," the school paper proclaimed in April 1951. Though the emphasis was on the positive applications of atomic energy, the students were not unaware of the dark side of the nuclear promise. That same year, one of the school's teachers, Miss Van Fleet, took a course in radiation monitoring in the event of thermonuclear war. Reporting on her reasons for enrolling in the course, Miss Van Fleet told *The Hollywood High School News* that "We should be prepared for an atomic attack for the same reason we take automobile insurance—not because we're hoping for an accident, but for protection in case of one." Given Hollywood High's early focus on the atomic age, it is perhaps fitting that one of its graduates holds the distinction of being the only person to witness the explosions of all three of the first atomic bombs. Laurence Johnston, class of 1935, was present at Alamogordo and set the charges on the bombs dropped over Hiroshima and Nagasaki.

Though the students attended the occasional assembly on the subject of atomic energy and participated in periodic drills in which they were led into sheltered areas and told to sit with their heads between their legs, there is no evidence that the possibility of nuclear devastation had any serious effect on Hollywood High's social scene in the early Fifties. Miss Hollywood was not dispensing advice on what to wear to World War III, but rather stressing the differences between the "in look" and the "out look." Angora sweaters were all the rage in those days: Any coed who did not possess one was by definition relegated to the "out" crowd. Saddle shoes and pageboy hairdos were also part of the fashionable look for girls, while the boys walked around in Levi's, T-shirts with rolled sleeves, and ducktail haircuts.

Popular after-school spots were the Orange Julius stand on Hollywood Boulevard, and Biff's, where Cokes were still a nickel. Every Friday night students had the choice of gathering either at the Hollywood High gym for the weekly "Coke sesh" or at the Hollywood Palladium for "teen night." (The latter was often the preference since it featured Harry James and the Dorsey Brothers.) In those days before rock 'n' roll, seventy percent of records were bought by people over twenty years of age. Singers like Perry Como, Eddie Fisher, Harry Belafonte, and Peggy Lee were popular; Rosemary Clooney was considered "wild." The jitterbug was still the conventional dance style.

As at most public high schools, students at Hollywood High had always congregated in well-defined cliques—those with parallel interests hanging out together. There were the actors, the scholars, the athletes, and so on, all of whom tended to segregate themselves from the general community. But the cliques seemed more powerful social forces in the Fifties. Back in the Twenties, the school's administration had strictly prohibited the organization of campus sororities and fraternities, out of a feeling that they would be divisive. That prohibition had been honored for decades. But by the Fifties, informal, unsanctioned groups, some with Greek names, existed at the school. One example was the Thetas sorority. The majority of the Thetas dated members of the school's football team. Thetas ate lunch together and had their own special hangouts. Nonmembers caught congregating in Theta territory were unceremoniously instructed to make themselves scarce.

Either as a result of or in spite of groups like the Thetas, Hollywood High's reputation as the school where the truly glamorous girls could be found had lost none of its luster. But the luster now had a certain lurid cast to it, at least in some eyes. By the early Fifties, a bit of the movie colony's aura of sin and sex (which was still being sensationalized by the fan magazines and tabloids) had inevitably rubbed off on Hollywood High. The school's femmes fatales were reputed to be faster and looser than their counterparts in neighboring schools, particularly Fairfax High, where the girls were thought of as goody-goodies. This was mostly hearsay, with very little foundation, most likely propagated by the Fairfax girls. In fact, Hollywood High's coeds were no looser than coeds anywhere else in the area, and that wasn't very loose at all, at least not by modern standards. The school had its "nice girls" and its "cheap girls." The latter wore earrings and straight skirts with no stockings, and smoked in the library bathroom. The former wore wool skirts and white bucks and brushed their hair in the library bathroom. Pregnancies were rare. "I remember one girl who got pregnant," says an alumnus from that era, "and we all thought she was a pretty dumb turkey."

Anything that the students didn't know about sex from their own experience, they were unlikely to learn at school. Sex education at Hollywood High in the early Fifties was meant to deter, not instruct. Science teachers administered the course, which consisted of showing a film to the students, who were segregated by gender for the occasion, lest they become too agitated by what appeared on the screen. What appeared on the screen was a bland documentary contrived by an oddly named firm called Erpy Classroom Films. The students promptly nicknamed them *Urp-ies*.

In her autobiography, *One More Time*, Carol Burnett (class of 1951) aptly described these less than graphic documentaries. "We'd see a happy, married couple smiling and doing happy-married things in their pretty little cottage," she wrote. "Her washing, and him drying ... her picking posies in the garden, and him watering the lawn ... her knitting, and him reading his paper and smoking his pipe ... then they'd look at each other and simply beam. Next, we'd be treated to some dumb animation about how the bees pollinate the flowers. And bang, before you know it, Mr. and Mrs. Happy are cuddling Hap Jr. and THE END pops up on the screen.... They did a better job than Ovaltine when it came to making me nod off in class."

2.

Sometimes a guy or two would ask me to jitterbug, but nine times out of ten, they were not only
a foot shorter than I was, but geeks to boot.

—Carol Burnett

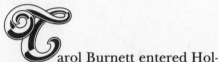arol Burnett entered Hol-
lywood High in 1949, having completed her course of
study at nearby Le Conte Junior High. *The Hollywood
High School News*, which customarily welcomed new students with a short write-up, offered this glowing account
of her Le Conte career: "Carol Burnett was editor of the
school newspaper, active in dramatics, and hopes to continue in these fields." Though smitten by the movies—as
a kid she used to scrape together the eleven-cent admission by scavenging neighborhood milk and soda bottles
for deposits—she was more directed toward journalism
than acting when she registered at Hollywood High.

Like most entering sophomores, young Carol was
somewhat awed by the prospect of going to Hollywood
High, a school widely considered to be the most famous
in America. Her first few weeks there were perhaps more
frightening than thrilling, however. This was a fairly
common reaction for new students accustomed to smaller
schools, for Hollywood High's enormous student population and mazelike complex of buildings (the school now
took up an entire city block) were enough to daunt even

the toughest fifteen-year-old. "I felt lost," Carol later recalled. "Stupid. Dumb. Outnumbered. Overwhelmed. Little. Insignificant."

Nevertheless, she must have overcome her insecurity in short order, for by March 1949 she was appointed to the rules and regulations committee by the president of the student body (the job required her to attend student council meetings), and by June she was appointed English department secretary, for which she was later awarded a silver pin. Though Spanish was her formal major, she excelled in English. That year the school paper even included her in its "Galloping Poll" column, something of an honor for an underclassman. The featured question was, "Who would you vote for in the election?" Carol's published reply: "Ah'm from Texas. We're thoroughbred Democrats down thaw!"

Unfortunately, Carol's social life was not quite as satisfying as her campus life. She would attend the Coke seshes and teen nights at the Hollywood Palladium, but true love, or the high school equivalent thereof, eluded her.

The odds were against her from the beginning. Her family, which had immigrated to Hollywood from San Antonio, Texas, in 1941, was poor and could not afford to buy Carol the kind of wardrobe sported by Hollywood High's stylish young fashion plates. (She could not even buy the obligatory angora sweater.) She was a gangly teenager and much too tall (five feet seven by age eleven). To make life even tougher, the female population of her class outnumbered the males, 219 to 184.

As a way of meeting the most popular boys, those on the football team, Carol signed up for the girls' drill team at the beginning of her junior year. The drill team's function was to march in various formations with the band at football games, and if nothing else, their uniforms—bright red corduroy jumpers, long-sleeved white blouses, red and white pom-poms—were conspicuous. To qualify for the team, which was a physical education elective, girls were judged on "personal appearance, rhythm, posture, and the ability to follow direction."

Unfortunately, Carol's tenure on the team was not destined to find her favor with the boys on the football squad. As she tells it, "That year, the Hollywood High girls' drill team had the reputation of being the worst in the entire Los Angeles high school district. And it was, too. Everybody in the bleachers either laughed at us, booed, or both. I dropped out before they started throwing things." Following the drill team fiasco, she joined the Girls' Athletic Association, where "every single one of the members outweighed me by a ton." She soon quit that activity, too, not long after the GAA's first after-school volleyball game.

By this time, Carol had joined the staff of the school paper and, by February of her junior year, was listed on the masthead as a reporter. Her first bylined article was entitled "School Electric Shop Offers to Repair Non-working Items." But she soon went on to ferret out livelier material, and the ingenuity of her reportorial technique was given its due in an item in the paper's gossip column, "Reflections in the Mirror": "We saw Carol Burnett peering through the keyhole of Miss Briggs' room and getting caught in the act," the item declared. "There must be an easier way to get news!"

Carol's career with the school paper brought her rec-

Carol Burnett (right) was editor in chief of the school newspaper her senior year, but all she really wanted out of life was to fall in love.

ognition and even a healthy degree of campus celebrity. In her senior year she was appointed editor in chief and, like all campus celebrities, duly became the subject of a school newspaper profile that assumed readers would want to know everything about her from her favorite food to her most exciting moment. "The reason Carol Burnett loves fried chicken," the front-page story began, "is probably because she's from the deep South.... Carol's suppressed desire is to call all teachers by their first names.... Her pet peeve is boys and girls who imitate their favorite actors and actresses and lose their own individuality." The article listed her greatest fault as stubbornness, her greatest extravagance as Cokes, and her greatest thrill as her first roller coaster ride at Ocean Park.

Carol edited the paper from February 1950 until her graduation in the winter of 1951. As part of her express commitment to livening up its drab pages, she introduced a series of interviews with Hollywood High alumni who had gone on to become movie stars. Naturally, she did the interviewing herself. The first of these was with Joel McCrea (who remembers her as being "a very charming youngster"), and she was about to complete her second, with Lana Turner, when the principal discovered that Carol was doing the interviews on class time. The series was promptly halted.

As editor, Carol was also the anonymous author of the popular "Roving I" column, one of the paper's regular features. "Roving I," purportedly penned by a sophomore, was a loose conglomeration of humorous poems and observations, many of which contained deliberate misspellings, the unifying conceit being that sopho-

mores, the lowest form of life on the school's evolution-
ary scale, could hardly be expected to know about proper
spelling or grammar—or anything else. It was one of the
first columns the kids read, and there was always great
speculation about the identity of the author, which was
kept secret. A few of Carol Burnett's "Roving I" entries
reveal an early talent for getting into character, for the
humor is nothing if not sophomoric—which was probably the secret of its success:

ETIKUT: Its sorta considered good taste when
you sorta bump sumone in the hall to go back
and pick 'em up.

EDITORIAL: People should be careful not to
stick their nose in other peoples business, because I got a black eye.

When you throw garbage in the quad always
be on the lookout because your lible to axiden-
tally hit a garbage can.

DAFFYNISHUN: (A SUCESFUL AMUMNY)
Everytime he opens his mouth he puts his feats
in it.

Carol's life improved immensely during her last year
at Hollywood High: She was writing the humor column,
her grades were excellent, and best of all, she had a boyfriend. His name was Gerry and he attended a local military school. He was, in her words, "gorgeous," and Carol
invited him to be her escort at the senior prom. That

year the prom committee pulled out all the stops and gave the event a nightclub theme. It was formal, of course, and each couple was greeted at the door of the gym by a student "waiter," who showed them to a table decorated with flowers, candles, and white tablecloth. Practically every boy wore either a tuxedo or a formal dinner jacket. Carol's ensemble, as reported by the school paper, was composed of "an old-fashioned black hoop skirt formal with white Irish lace trimmings and gloves."

Carol Burnett enrolled at UCLA the following September, set on pursuing her journalism career. At the time, however, the college did not offer an undergraduate journalism course, so Carol ended up majoring in dramatics with the aim of becoming a playwright. It was at UCLA, not Hollywood High, that her on-stage talents would became apparent, and soon after she got there, she dropped play-writing in favor of acting. The rest, as they say, is history.

3.

Three ways to avoid embarrassment when you fall on the dance floor:

1. Just lie there—they'll think you fainted.

2. Get up gracefully—they'll think it's part of the dance.

3. Start mopping the floor with your handkerchief—they'll think you work there.

—*The Hollywood High School*
News, 1953

eanwhile, the competition provided by television was still confounding the studios. The new medium was growing at an alarming rate, and programming was improving. Such shows as *Dragnet* and *I Love Lucy* became available to TV viewers in 1952, and the networks were now broadcasting coast to coast. More and more people were staying home and watching the tube.

Most studio executives agreed that in order to compete with television, movies had to offer something new and different. By new and different they did not necessarily mean better movies; they meant bigger movies. The first result of this conclusion was Cinerama, an extrawide-screen system requiring three projectors in every theatre and a multitude of speakers. It was not a big success: The music was deafeningly loud, the actors on the edge of the screen were often distorted, and most exhibitors couldn't afford all the extra equipment. CinemaScope, which came next, was basically Cinerama on a slightly smaller scale. It solved some of the distortion problems, but there were difficulties with close-up shots since the process was designed primarily for big-cast spectaculars. VistaVision solved the close-up problems but, like Cinerama, was too expensive for theatre owners.

But the studios' most memorable answer to television was the 3D movie, or "deepie" as it was originally called. Moviegoers were required to wear Polaroid glasses to get the three-dimensional effect. Skeptics opined that 3D films would fail because viewers would never be persuaded to wear the glasses. To this a Paramount executive replied, "They'll wear toilet seats around their necks if you give 'em what they want to see!"

Deepies were launched in November 1952 with an epic called *Bwana Devil*. The plot, which involved a group of hungry man-eating lions who attempt to dine on a crew of African railroad workers, was generally panned, but the film grossed ninety-five thousand dollars its first week in release. Hollywood rejoiced, thinking it had finally found an antidote to television. But the novelty wore off fast, and within a year, movies shot in 3D were also being offered in "flat" versions. One of these was Alfred Hitchcock's *Dial M for Murder*, which was shot in 3D but distributed flat in 1954. "A nine-day wonder," Hitchcock said of the 3D sensation, "and I came in on the ninth day."

The 3D craze was only a fleeting sensation at Hollywood High, and there is little mention of it in the school paper. "We were always up for anything new," recalls one alumnus. "Some of the kids would wear their three-D glasses to school, but that didn't last long. There was one film in which an actor actually spat at the audience, and that got everybody talking because it was so disgusting, but the general attitude about three-D was that if you'd seen one, you'd seen them all."

Of much more interest to the typical Hollywood High student of that era was the souped-up hot rod. The streets surrounding the school—Sunset, Highland, and Hollywood Boulevard—had become informal motoramas, with students proudly displaying their embellished, mutated vehicles and unabashedly screeching their tires for effect. "When a teenager tears up a street with car exhausts blasting," the school paper scolded, "he may think he is impressing the girl he is taking home from school, but what kind of impression is he making on the people who walk along the boulevard?" By popular demand, Hollywood High's first annual hot rod show was held on the football field in November 1954, and it was a roaring success. Entries that year included a 1951 Chevy Bel-Air (with louvered hood, shaved trunk, and forty coats of two-tone paint) and a '47 Mercury (with rechromed bumpers and refrenched headlights).

Cars were known as *wheels* in those days as new slang terms entered the teen vocabulary. What had been *hot* in the late Forties was now *cool*. Teens could take their wheels to a *passion pit* on Friday night unless they'd been *grounded* by Mom and Dad. School was a *drag*, and it was considered *cool* to *hang loose*. Though there were no *beatniks* to be found on the Hollywood High campus, students could wander down to Venice Beach on weekends to observe these oddly dressed, bearded types who talked of Zen and listened to jazz. Venice Beach was considered the western headquarters of what would later be known as the Beat Generation.

Also considered cool was rock 'n' roll, a new kind of music which was beginning to replace the more conventional sounds of Perry Como and Tony Bennett. "Rock Around the Clock," as sung by Bill Haley and the Comets, was a big favorite at Hollywood High in 1955, and only a few campus "squares" missed Elvis Presley's 1956 appearance on the *Ed Sullivan Show*. A number of musically inclined students even formed their own combos and played at school dances and proms. The most famous of these was the Four Preps, a quartet of Hollywood High students, one of whom was Glen Larson, today a successful producer. It may be purely coincidental, but Hollywood High's academic standing began to slip slightly around the same time that rock 'n' roll took hold of the campus. In 1956, with Elvis Presley's "Don't Be Cruel" chalking up a huge majority as the student body's favorite record and a column titled "Platter Chatter" debuting in the pages of the school paper, results of the Iowa Test scores showed the school's seniors scoring in the eightieth percentile in math and the eighty-ninth percentile in literature. Though scores in vocabulary and social studies were better—ninety-fifth and ninety-eighth respectively—the relatively weak math and English scores were deemed unsatisfactory by the administration, and a greater homework load was mandated.

By 1957 only the stalwart goody-goodies who wrote editorials for the school paper were still bothering to bewail the pervasive influence of rock 'n' roll—everybody else was bebopping. "It is true," a 1957 editorial chided, "that many adults today think the female teenager is a wild, boy-crazy thing, slouching around the corner drug-store, that the male is a loud lout in blue suede shoes, and their worthlessness is expressed in that disgusting music form beneath contempt, rock 'n' roll. This conception is contradicted by the fact that 8,000,000 young people are now studying a musical instrument and even more participate in organized choral groups and in high school bands."

4.

It took me until the twelfth grade before I even
thought that someone would think I was pretty.
— Sally Kellerman

n 1953 Hollywood High
celebrated its fiftieth anniversary with a number of student assemblies and alumni celebrations. The festivities
were somewhat muted, however, because of the recent
death of Dr. William Snyder, who had brought so much
fame and honor to Hollywood High. As many of the anniversary speakers noted, Doc Snyder would be sorely
missed.

The following year, Louis Foley retired after twenty-
five years as principal. He was replaced at the beginning
of the new semester by Harold E. Perry, principal of Ver-
dugo Hills High School and a former assistant park nat-
uralist at Yosemite. "I want everyone to know that my
door is always open, even if it's just for a friendly visit,"
Perry declared in the school paper upon taking up the
reins of his new office.

One of principal Perry's first responsibilities would
be the appointment of a new drama instructor. In 1949,
after a memorable thirty-year term as Hollywood High's
drama director, Arthur Kachel had retired. Over the next
two or three years, since a replacement had not been

named, Kaich was brought back to direct an occasional production—several operettas and a number of Christmas programs. It was not until 1955 that Perry hired a permanent replacement, a young man named John Ingle.

Though Arthur Kachel was a hard act for any man to follow, Ingle, a Navy veteran and graduate of Occidental College, did not allow the reputation of his highly esteemed predecessor to daunt him. "Sure, there was still this aura about him and how I'd never fill his shoes," Ingle recalled, "but it was never really articulated, and I didn't let it affect me." Ingle soon proved himself a worthy successor—during his nine-year stint as Hollywood High's drama director, he would maintain the high caliber of the school's award-winning drama department and become an inspiration to such teenage talents as Barbara Hershey, Swoosie Kurtz, Linda Evans, Stefanie Powers, and Meredith Baxter Birney, in much the same way Arthur Kachel had been to budding stars of earlier decades.

During the mid-Fifties (roughly 1954 through 1957) Hollywood High experienced a sudden surge in its output of student talent. If the late Forties and early Fifties had been fairly lackluster, by 1955 the campus was virtually crawling with would-be stars.

The class of 1954 started the ball rolling with David Nelson, son of Ozzie and Harriet, brother of Ricky. Young Dave Nelson was already something of a celebrity by the time he arrived at Hollywood High, having been a regular player on the *Adventures of Ozzie and Harriet* radio show since 1948, and on the television version since 1952. Somehow he managed to juggle his frequent radio and TV appearances with homework and an active participation in school athletics. Sports, in fact, were Dave's passion at school, and he played quarterback on the B football team his sophomore year, a season in which Hollywood High won six out of six and captured the Western League Championship. During his senior year, he was tailback on the varsity, swam backstroke on the swimming team, and pitched for the varsity baseball squad. Ozzie Nelson recalled one of his son's less outstanding moments on the Hollywood High baseball diamond: "One afternoon, I decided to swing around to Hollywood High . . . so that I could watch a couple of innings of a game Dave was playing in. As luck would have it, he was just coming to bat as I turned the corner. I was almost a block away, but he recognized the car and waved to me and then smashed a long drive up against the fence for what was obviously an 'inside-the-park' home run. I headed back to the studio to spread the good news, and he waved to me once again as he circled the bases. When he arrived on the set about an hour later, Harriet rushed over to congratulate him. 'Dad told us about the home run,' she said. 'Only one thing though,' said David gloomily, 'it wasn't a home run. I was so busy waving to Dad I forgot to touch second base.' "

The most memorable moment of Dave Nelson's high school baseball career came during a game that Hollywood High lost to Van Nuys High his senior year. It would have been a no-hitter for the Van Nuys pitcher if Dave hadn't scored a single in the last inning. Though Dave's base hit couldn't save the day for his teammates, he can still be proud to have scored one against the Van Nuys pitcher, who has since gone on to stardom himself—none other than Don Drysdale.

Dave Nelson was not the class of 1954's only contribution to the entertainment industry. That year a diploma was also handed out to actress Ruta Lee, whose film credits include *Marjorie Morningstar, Sergeants 3,* and *Witness for the Prosecution.* On campus she was known as Ruta Kilmonis (of Lithuanian descent), and her high school life was an active one. She danced in many school productions, performed a solo in the Spring Music–Dance Festival, made the honor roll a number of times, and staged and starred in Hollywood High's production of *Naughty Marietta* her senior year. Like many aspiring starlets before her, Ruta Lee had been well aware of the school's reputation and attended Hollywood High with the express idea of being discovered à la Lana Turner, or, as she tells it in her studio publicity bio, "By the time I was 11, I knew I wanted to get into the movies. Fortunately, Dad had enough property to give in graciously, cash in, and move us all West, so I could go to Hollywood High and start sipping sodas at Schwab's."

Sally Kellerman (class of 1955) also came to Hollywood High with hopes of being discovered and spent most of her lunch hours and much of her lunch money at the same nearby soda fountain that Lana Turner had frequented. But in Sally's case, the only thing that came of it was that she got a little "pudgy."

Sally Kellerman's stretch at Hollywood High was similar to Carol Burnett's. Both girls turned into campus activists after a difficult period of adjustment, and both felt unsuccessful at one of high school's most highly valued rites of passage: the dating game. Sally's family had moved from the San Fernando Valley over the hill to Hollywood during her freshman year, and young Sally felt uprooted, lonely, and out of place among the school's

221

Sally Kellerman (far right) played the part of "Mother" in Hollywood High's 1955 production of *Meet Me in St. Louis.*

made-up, high-heeled coeds. "My first month at Hollywood High," she later reminisced, "I spent in solitude, crestfallen because I had accidentally sat on the club bench of one of the more exclusive groups and one of the girls had made an unkind remark. In those days, I was a loser. I was self-conscious because I wasn't like everybody else. I was tall (5'10"); I was a hick in a class of sophisticates; a refugee from the saddle shoes, butch haircuts and horse clubs of the Valley, among girls who were sleek and glamorous and who wore makeup and high heeled shoes."

To conceal her self-consciousness, Sally became somewhat eccentric and took to singing to herself as she walked about the campus. Her classmates interpreted this to mean she was perpetually cheerful—precisely what she wanted them to believe—but in actuality she was miserable. To further keep the false image alive, she became something of a class clown.

Insecurities aside, young Sally Kellerman was a joiner, for the 1955 *Poinsettia* credits her with memberships in such school activities as the Orchesis Club, the National Forensic League, the Inter-Club Council, and the yearbook staff. As for the single most important extracurricular activity—dating—it, unfortunately, was not one of her strong points. Though she was voted one of the most popular girls on campus, young Sally Kellerman was hardly ever asked out on a date.

Though becoming an actress and falling in love were the two things she wanted most from her high school career, she never landed a steady boyfriend, nor did she even go to tryouts for school plays until her last year at Hollywood High. To her way of thinking, going out for

223

a play was tantamount to admitting she was pretty, and Sally was much too insecure about her looks to consider herself thespian material. But by her senior year she finally got up the gumption to take the plunge, and promptly landed a plum role in Hollywood's High's production of *Meet Me in St. Louis*. She played the mother, Mrs. Smith, described in the school paper as "an attractive woman in her 40's with a gentle firm manner." Sally later claimed, with characteristic self-deprecation, that the only reason she got the role was because she was the tallest in the group.

Sally Kellerman's yearbook picture shows her, still with a butch haircut, staring dreamily up at the sky. Following graduation in 1955, she went to New York to attend the Actor's Studio. She made her film debut in the 1959 camp classic *Reform School Girl*, but it wasn't until 1969, when Robert Altman chose her to play the character of Major "Hot Lips" Houlihan in the film version of *M*A*S*H*, that her career began to take off.

M*A*S*H was also instrumental in giving Mike Farrell, class of 1957, his first major exposure to audiences (as Captain B. J. Hunnicut in the television series adapted from the film). A native of South St. Paul, Minnesota, Farrell grew up in Los Angeles, the son of a movie studio carpenter, and graduated from Bancroft Junior High (where he served as president of the student council) to Hollywood High in 1954.

Farrell remembers his years at Hollywood High as "a really good time. I was a member of a group of guys called the Saracens. Most of us had gone to Bancroft Junior High, where we called ourselves the Banshees, and we hung out together. We used to have meetings and

The class of 1957's Mike Farrell (seated, center) was head cheerleader his senior year, but spent much of his spare time cruising Hollywood Boulevard and looking cool.

parties and drag races, and sometimes we'd cruise Hollywood Boulevard and act tough." But despite the tough exterior, Mike managed to steer clear of detention study hall. "I was never a troublemaker, and I don't remember ever being in any real hot water. There was a lot of beer drinking going on within the student body in those days and a few fights and rumbles, but compared to today, it was a very tame period. In those days, having a joint was considered pretty extreme."

After school, when he wasn't cruising the boulevard or acting tough, Farrell worked—for a time as a paper-boy, then as a delivery boy for a grocery store. For a brief period he played the trumpet in the school band, and was a member of the track team his sophomore year. Scholastically, he managed to maintain a fairly solid B average. "I was a lazy student," he says. "I don't remember being challenged by any particular subject. I managed to get B's in algebra and a C in geometry. One year I had to take a speech class and was terrified the whole semester." Stage fright also kept him from pursuing his acting dreams. "I never even set foot in drama class," he confesses. "I was terrified of the very idea. I had strong acting ambitions but I didn't tell anybody."

Socially, young Mike Farrell followed the prevailing teenage codes of conduct, most important of which was the need to maintain one's cool under all circumstances. "Cool was chasing girls and cruising Hollywood Boulevard. Square was the Debate club, or anything we were too scared to do. At dances, we mostly used to stand around a lot. Some people actually had the courage to dance, but most of us just stood in corners trying to look cool. I think by the eleventh grade I finally got up the courage to ask a girl to dance." Farrell suffered his share of unfulfilled crushes: "I spent most of my high school years being in love with girls who were totally inaccessible to me—I suppose it was safer that way. I dated a couple of girls on a regular basis but I never went steady."

Though Mike Farrell does not remember ever holding student office during his three-year stint at Hollywood High, the record shows that he was elected president of his junior class in 1955. He does recall, with more than a little embarrassment, an honor that was bestowed upon him the following year: heading up the cheerleading squad. Since the early days at Hollywood High, the cheerleading squad had been exclusively male. Originally called "yell leaders," the boys maintained their hold on this activity until the Sixties, so that the female half of the population could aspire only to "pom-pom girl" status. Thus it came to pass that during his senior year, Mike Farrell was able to hold the position of head cheerleader. The job called for him to lead the fans in rousing cheers and loyalty songs, and surely it must have been considered cool at the time or young Mike wouldn't have accepted the position.

The class of 1957 also produced three actresses and a rock singer. Performing in a Hollywood High dance recital, Donna Anderson was discovered by director Stanley Kramer and subsequently cast in *On the Beach* and *Inherit the Wind*. Her classmate, Cynthia Pepper, also deeply involved in Hollywood High's dramatic activities, went on to star in the successful television series *Margie*. And Louise Sorel, known as Louise Cohen in those days,

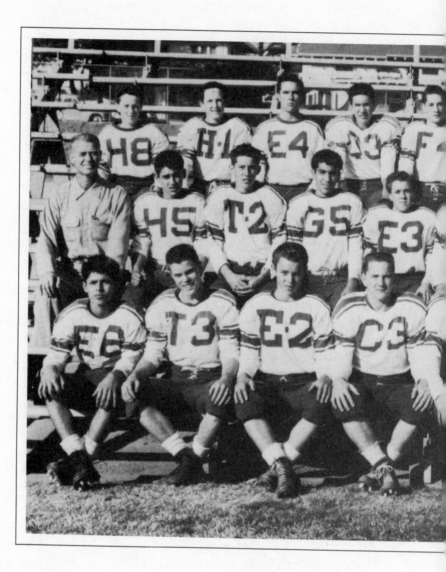

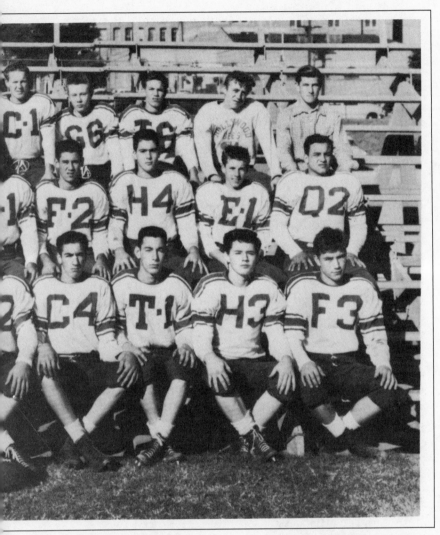

Ricky Nelson (second row, second from the right) played on the B football team until a broken hand sidelined him.

was featured in such films as *B.S. I Love You* and *Plaza Suite* before she gained wider fame in daytime soap operas.

As for the rock singer—like his brother Dave, Rick Nelson was already a celebrity when he registered at Hollywood High in the fall of 1954, having appeared regularly on his parents' television show since its debut in 1952. Viewers of the program knew him only as cute "Little Ricky," the Nelsons' youngest son, for the rock 'n' roll bug had not yet bitten him. Taking after his older brother, young Ricky made sports his first priority when he got to Hollywood High, and he managed to make the B football team his sophomore year even though his slight weight (115 pounds) nearly disqualified him. He played valiantly for a while but was eventually sidelined with a broken hand. From the bench he watched his teammates suffer one of their worst seasons ever. That year the B squad lost six out of eight games.

Like brother Dave, Rick managed to juggle homework, sports, and a regular acting stint with the aid of a studio tutor. Once the broken hand had healed, he tore up the tennis courts, winning numerous interscholastic tennis tournaments, and ultimately placing fifth in the Southern California fifteen-and-under division.

Perhaps because of his somewhat sporadic attendance at school, his name does not appear often in the pages of *The News*. One item that does feature him ran in the March 1955 issue of the paper. Rick was approached by the student pollsters who collected responses for a regular column entitled "Question of the Week." The question was: "What do you think of high school students going dutch on some of their dates or of girls paying part of the expenses?" Rick's answer was terse but sensible: "If the girl can afford it, she should help out a little."

Most of his classmates and teachers remember Rick Nelson as an affable kid with a crew cut. "He was an average student," one of his English teachers recalls, "and a friendly youngster." Though Mike Farrell and Rick Nelson knew each other at Hollywood High, they were not close friends, if for no other reason than that they were a semester apart and it was considered uncool for upperclassmen to fraternize too closely with underclassmen. "He was not revered as some special entity because of his status in the industry," Farrell reflects. "After all, it was not that far from the norm at Hollywood High."

It was while he was still a student at Hollywood High that Rick Nelson really began his career as a rock singer. Like most kids, he had played musical instruments as part of his education from an early age. He had taken clarinet lessons as a grade school student and later performed on the drums for his parents' TV show. With the advent of rock 'n' roll, he took up the guitar, too, practicing chords in his home bathroom, where the tiles provided the best acoustics. But it was one of his Hollywood High girlfriends who inadvertently convinced him to become a singer. As the story goes, the girl was madly infatuated with Elvis Presley and not especially impressed by her young boyfriend's drum playing and guitar strumming. Rick's pride was hurt and he decided there and then to give singing a try. Shortly thereafter, his first record, "I'm Walkin'," sold a million copies within its first week of release.

Though Rick Nelson had registered as a member of

the class of 1957, he did not receive his Hollywood High diploma until June 1959. His sudden new fame as a singer and his continuing appearances on *The Adventures of Ozzie and Harriet* caused him to miss most of his classes his senior year, and the remainder of his education was administered by tutors. Nevertheless, he always regarded Hollywood High as his alma mater, and in June 1981 he returned to the campus to perform a special benefit concert for the school's performing arts fund.

Friday night slumber party—watched *Mickey Mouse Club*, played bongo drums, and nibbled on cold enchiladas. Listened to Harry Belafonte's "Calypso for People Who Hate Calypso," gossiped about girls who were not there, discussed our favorite subjects: boys, clothes, boys, movies, boys, food, boys ..."

—From a *Hollywood High School News* article on a typical day in the life of a Hollywood High coed.

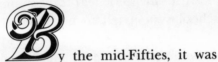y the mid-Fifties, it was apparent that the studios would survive television. Although thirty-two million American households now had TV, people were getting tired of sitting home in front of the box and once again longed for a night out at the movies. Box office receipts began to show signs of recovery as early as 1954. Profits may not have been as lofty as they were during the war years, but there was a definite uptick to the graph.

Around this time the studios finally began to realize that their interests could be served by making their products (movies) and their facilities (sound stages) available to television. For a price, of course. Columbia Pictures led the way by being the first studio to sell feature films to the networks. The other majors soon jumped on the bandwagon, and more profits were forthcoming. Everybody was happy.

As for the rest of the population, the last half of the

decade was a period characterized by a multitude of fears and anxieties, none of which had much to do with either moviemaking or television production. There was the fear of polio, an epidemic that ravaged Hollywood High with the same ferocity as elsewhere in the nation. A campaign to vaccinate nine hundred thousand people in the area was taken up by the school newspaper. In March 1957 inoculations were given to anyone with parental approval. "The shot hurts no more than a pin prick," the paper declared. "Are you going to join the bandwagon and be vaccinated?"

Also in 1957 fear of Communists infiltrating the school system led to a lively debate over the efficacy of signed loyalty oaths. "The idealist who is so self-righteously shocked by the thought of having to sign a loyalty oath is merely playing into the hands of the Communists," was the reasoning of the pro-oath contingent, while the opposition claimed that Communists will sign anything.

Sputnik caused Hollywood High to reappraise its entire scholastic curriculum, with particular attention being paid to the science and math departments. "Our educational system has been under closer scrutiny than at any time in the history of education," the school paper warned in 1957. "When the Russians launched their Sputnik, we were rudely shocked at the inadequacy of our science and mathematical achievements." Hollywood High responded to the challenge by increasing its math and science requirements. The homework load grew again.

Sputnik also gave birth to Hollywood High's first rocket club, a conglomeration of young Wernher von

Brauns whose objective was to design, construct, and launch a rocket. Unfortunately, the initial efforts of the new club were somewhat less than inspiring. By the autumn of 1957 the club members had built their first deployable rocket ship. Seven feet in length, two and one half inches in diameter, it weighed seventy pounds and held thirty pounds of fuel. November 30 was the launch date, and the club members all gathered breathlessly at a spot in the Mojave Desert to watch their model soar to the heavens. The countdown began. The fuel was ignited. The rocket burst into smithereens on the launchpad.

An autopsy later revealed that one of the craft's nozzles had malfunctioned, but the president of the club managed to put the best possible face on the catastrophe by saying, "Although our first attempt was a failure as far as altitude performance is concerned, we have learned a great deal." Members of the club were later invited to appear as special guests on *The Mickey Mouse Club*.

PART SIX

1.

We're not nasty; we're not mean; we'll give a cheer
for the other team: M-I-C-K-E-Y M-O-U-S-E!
　　　　　　　　　—New football cheer, 1961

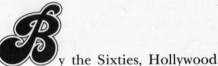y the Sixties, Hollywood
was no longer the true home of the motion picture in-
dustry. Only sporadic location shooting was done in the
area, and many of the studios were headquartered in
other parts of Los Angeles. Disney, Universal, and
Warner Bros. had moved to cheaper, more spacious lots
in the San Fernando Valley (Columbia would follow in
1972); 20th Century-Fox was in West L.A.; the MGM lot
was in Culver City. NBC had located its headquarters in
Burbank, and CBS shot most of its programs on the old
Republic Studios lot in Studio City. Only Paramount remained at its old Melrose Avenue address.

Moreover, most of the big stars had long since moved
to more fashionable locales like Brentwood and Beverly
Hills. Some maintained huge ranches or farms in the San
Fernando Valley. In the early Fifties these huge lots were
subdivided into residential tracts and the area began to
lure many ordinary Hollywoodians who had grown tired
of their city's congestion and high real estate prices. The
completion of the first leg of the Hollywood Freeway in

239

1951 turned the Valley into Los Angeles's fastest-growing suburban mecca.

It would be a while before Hollywood would begin to suffer noticeably from the vacuum. In 1960, despite the loss of so much local wealth, the community was still a nice place to live. The streets were being torn up for the 1,558 coral terrazzo stars that would comprise the Hollywood "Walk of Fame"—the Chamber of Commerce's attempt to bring some of the glamour back to Hollywood—but a nighttime stroll down Hollywood Boulevard was still a pleasant experience. Commerce was lively and the movie palaces were packed on Saturday nights. On weekends, teens from Hollywood High would still cruise the Boulevard in their souped-up cars or take in a movie followed by a pizza and Coke at McGoo's. The city's populace was not as wealthy as it had been before, but there were no real pockets of poverty either. Hollywood in 1960 was still a community of normal, middle-class families. It was, however, still hopelessly congested. As new, less affluent families moved into the city, single-family dwelling, were converted into apartments.

Since you didn't have to live in Hollywood to attend Hollywood High, the school's population continued to rise. By 1960, it stood at twenty-three hundred, an unwieldy number that prompted principal Perry to employ two emergency measures to curb the campus population explosion. No more permits to attend Hollywood High would be issued to students living outside the district—a practice that had prevailed throughout much of the school's history. Moreover, students whose attitudes toward school were found unsatisfactory would be "eased out into their parents' custody." In other words, there would be no room at Hollywood High for habitual truants and juvenile delinquents. Not that there were many. Like most American secondary schools of the era, Hollywood High had a fringe element of hoods and toughs, but these were strictly a minority. By and large the students remained a serious, wholesome lot, clean-cut and conscientious. The senior class of 1960 not only produced thirteen National Merit Finalists but saw three of its members ranked among the top high school English students in the nation.

At a time when the pressures on the college-bound had never been more intense, and the post-Sputnik panic about catching up with the Russians was still in the air, the homework load continued to be sizable. One campus wit, writing in the pages of *The Hollywood High School News*, suggested two proven methods for completing homework with a minimum of strain. There was the "electric method": "In a rainy lightning storm, simply stuff your notes into a long pole (which you hold high above your head), take off your shoes and stand in a knee-deep puddle of water. Soon in a flash, wisdom will flow through you." The other system was the "beat method," in which you "must tear up all your assignments, put them in the fireplace with a full box of incense, light the fire, and do a handstand with your feet against the door."

Meanwhile, the social scene was undergoing changes. Surfing was beginning to take hold as a campus craze, and the sight of surfboards tied to car roofs was fast becoming a common sight in Southern California. At first, local parents (including those of many Hollywood High students) disapproved of the sport, equating surfers with dropouts and bums who wandered aimlessly on the beach. But a modicum of acceptance came with the release of the movie *Gidget* in 1960, which gave surfing national exposure and made its champions overnight celebrities.

Not everyone at Hollywood High surfed, but practically everyone embraced the new surfing culture which swept the area. Surfing music began with "Surfer Stomps," informal California dances featuring the sounds of groups like Dick Dale and the Del-Tones. The Beach Boys soon dominated the craze with their first surfing hit, "Surfin' Safari," in 1962. Though many serious surfers deplored the Beach Boys because their succession of hit songs resulted in overcrowded beaches, such tunes as "Surfin' USA" and "Wipe Out" by the Surfaris were megahits at Hollywood High. Surfing also created new fashions: Madras shirts, chinos, sweatshirts, and windbreakers became popular on campus. Panel trucks could be seen in the school's parking lot. (Real surfers, of course, did not drive woodies—they hauled themselves and their boards to the beach in panel trucks.) And surfing also fostered a whole new language: "gremmies" and "kooks" were beginners; "boss" meant "great"; and "Cowabunga" was surf talk for "Wow!"

Surfing may have been the era's biggest fad, but it was hardly the only one to grip the campus. The early Sixties saw the appearance of such manias as hot dogs on a stick, yo-yos, and a number of new dances such as the moe kay, the coffee grind, the slop, the twist, the gully, and the limbo ("not really a dance, but a demonstration of physical skill done to music," the ever helpful school newspaper clarified). The boys still had relatively short hair, but the girls were starting to sport such elaborately styled coiffures as the beehive, the bouffant, the

2.

I grew up near a drugstore where a lot of movie
stars dropped in. When I was a kid I thought
nothing of sitting at the soda counter alongside
Burt Lancaster or Fred MacMurray. Sometimes
Ava Gardner came in to buy lipsticks.

—Stefanie Powers

ollywood High's reputa-
tion as a proving ground for future screen stars remained very much intact throughout the Sixties. Talented
students were still in abundance, on-campus discovery
was still a possibility, school productions maintained
their professional caliber, and the glamour of the surrounding neighborhood—Hollywood Boulevard in particular—had not yet completely faded. Subsequent years
would produce only a smattering of student talent—
mostly minor TV performers—leading most school
historians to agree that the decade of the Sixties was Hollywood High's last hurrah.

John Ingle's able stewardship of the school's drama
department is at least part of the reason for the impressive surge of talent from 1960 through 1964 (the year he
left)—a period comparable to the glory years of the Thirties. Like his predecessor, Ingle chose each semester's
production ("plays with large casts were my usual preference, but I tried to keep a balance") and ran a tight
ship when it came to rehearsals. "There was no play
time," he says. "You just came to rehearsal and that was

that. The theatrical discipline was never lax, and I don't recall ever having to punish anyone, because the kids simply never missed rehearsals. Hollywood High was the top of the heap in drama, and our standards were very high." Auditions were competitive, for some sixty percent of Ingle's drama students intended to pursue acting as a profession.

The decade began with the graduation of two of Hollywood High's most celebrated graduates. As members of the class of 1960, Stefanie Powers and Linda Evans were classmates, but though they knew each other slightly at school—rumor has it they even fought over the attentions of the same boy at one time—their high school careers were anything but similar.

Stefanie Powers was born in Hollywood in 1942 and, as a youngster, took the obligatory ballet lessons at a local dance school whose other pupils included such pre-adolescent cutie-pies as Natalie Wood and Jill St. John. Her given name—Stefania Zofia Federkiewicz—was practically unpronounceable, and by the time she got to high school she was known simply as Taffy Paul. Paul was her mother's maiden name; the nickname Taffy, first applied by her brother, was derived from one of the characters on the radio serial *Terry and the Pirates*.

By her own admission, Taffy Paul was a mediocre student, painfully bored by her classes at Hollywood High. Her favorite subjects were science and the arts, but young Taffy was far more interested in extracurricular activities, sports, and the occasional campus prank. Her junior year, she joined the girls' drill team, which had cleaned up its act somewhat since Carol Burnett's time. She was also one of the school's most popular pom-pom

Stefanie Powers's yearbook picture, 1960. In those days she was familiarly known as "Taffy Paul."

girls (boys were still officially the cheerleaders), a member of the chess club, and a participant in Hollywood High's student exchange program, though she never studied abroad. Swimming was her best sport and she was elected captain of the girls' swimming team her senior year.

Unlike many of her classmates, young Taffy Paul was not particularly star-struck during her high school years. Having grown up in Hollywood, she was accustomed to seeing stars and starlets hanging around the local drugstore or driving down Sunset Boulevard. The glamour of the movie business did not fill her with anything approaching awe. Nevertheless, she tried out for productions, but was never selected for any major roles. It was as a dancer that she made her mark. When the school put on a musical variety show called *Stage-o-rama '60,* Taffy Paul, then a senior, was one of fifty-two girls selected to sing and dance to numbers from *Oklahoma, Showboat, South Pacific,* and *West Side Story.*

Taffy Paul also admits to having had a gift for rowdyism. One particular incident stands out: As a prank, she and a few of her friends chopped down a campus tree. "It was a fairly big tree, and it 'belonged' to one of the rival campus sororities," recalls Hollywood High's former principal, Willard Hansen, who was then an English teacher. "These sororities were not authorized by the school, but they sprang up anyway. There was a lot of rivalry, of course." Taffy and her band of marauders were hauled away by the police. She recalled her brief visit to the local precinct for *People* magazine in 1982: "There we were, all these lily white kids with crew cuts and tennis shoes sitting down there like we were on a field trip, surrounded by kids who were in juvenile hall for robbery, assault, burglaries. It was all pretty silly."

Though not deeply committed to the idea of a movie career, Taffy Paul did recognize at an early age that film work paid extremely well. Thus, at the age of fifteen, she auditioned for a part in the movie version of *West Side Story* and was selected, from a large group of dancers, as one of the Jets. She must have lied about her age, however, because after three months of rehearsals, when it was discovered that she was underage, she was immediately dismissed from the cast. Following graduation, when her age was no longer a concern, she was given a small role in the movie *Tammy Tell Me True,* and subsequently signed to a contract by Columbia Pictures.

By contrast, Linda Evans was far less self-assured than Taffy Paul during her years at Hollywood High. Both girls were graced with youthful good looks, but Linda Evans was quieter, more introverted, and certainly not possessed of Taffy's mischievous spirit. In fact, it was for the purpose of overcoming her extreme self-consciousness that she signed up for drama classes and joined the Orchesis Club. John Ingle remembers her as "a lovely girl, but very quiet and quite shy."

She was born in Hartford, Connecticut, the daughter of professional dancers who moved to Los Angeles when Linda was six months old. Her name in those days was not Evans but Evenstad. After classes at Hollywood High and sometimes on Saturdays, she earned pocket money by working as an usherette at the nearby Paramount Theatre. As a teenager, she dated only two boys, one of whom broke her heart by marrying another girl. While most of her friends had parentally imposed curfews, Linda's par-

Linda Evans (née Evanstad) as she appeared in her year-book, 1960. Rumor has it she and classmate Stefanie Powers fought over the same boy.

ents left the responsibility of coming home at a reason-
able hour up to their daughter. Young Linda never
violated their trust. "I must have been the oldest virgin
in Hollywood," she confessed to the *Ladies' Home Journal.*

During her junior year the Hollywood High Girls
League decided to put on a gala fashion show in front
of the entire student body, and both Linda Evenstad and
Taffy Paul were chosen by a panel of teachers to be
among the thirty coed models. By this time Linda had
conquered at least some of her stage fright. Sportswear,
formals, and bathing suits were modeled in the auditorium. The bathing suits received the most tumultuous
applause.

Though she attended drama classes at Hollywood
High, Linda Evenstad was never chosen for any of the
school plays. Her introduction to show business occurred
by accident. One of her best friends at school was a girl
named Carole Wells, who had appeared in several small
movie roles and later went on to star in the television
series *National Velvet.* Carol had an audition for a Can-
ada Dry commercial one afternoon and convinced her
friend Linda to accompany her. While Carol read for the
part, Linda sat quietly in a corner observing the audition,
but her good looks attracted the eye of the casting agent,
who ended up offering her a part in the commercial. "I
was shocked when they wanted me to do that commercial," Linda recalled. "I couldn't believe it. All through
high school I felt that I was dreadful-looking. And I actually had kind of mousy brown hair. I just wanted to
blend in with the wall. I didn't want anyone to notice me
too much because I was very shy." Shortly after graduation day, MGM signed her to a contract, and several of

her first TV roles had her costarring with such Hollywood High alumni as Richard Long (in *The Big Valley*) and David and Rick Nelson (in *Ozzie and Harriet*).

Today Linda Evans looks back at her high school career as one of the less memorable periods of her life. Twenty-two years after she received her sheepskin, a newspaper reporter asked her if she'd done anything outstanding at Hollywood High. Linda Evans's terse reply was: "I graduated."

Which is more than Tuesday Weld can say. If she had graduated, she would have celebrated the occasion with the class of 1961. But her tenure at Hollywood High is noted primarily for its brevity—she lasted less than one week, outstripping even Lana Turner for swiftest passage through those hallowed halls.

Tuesday Weld had begun acting in films at the age of twelve—*Rock, Rock, Rock* was her first—and most of her education was conducted on various studio lots. Between films she would be enrolled in public schools, most of which she despised. A heavy smoker and drinker by fourteen, she was known around town as a kooky teen with a pronounced tendency toward rebellion. At the ripe old age of fifteen, she confessed to feeling like an adult, particularly around teenage girls who giggled childishly over boys.

Her brief Hollywood High residency was an experience she would never forget. "Nobody paid any attention to me at all the first day I went to school," Tuesday remembers, "so the second day I got all dressed in black— black dress, black hat, long black gloves, black shoes. Oh boy, did I get attention. The principal told me to go home and change. I was causing such a riot."

Willard Hansen remembers the incident: "I was working in the office the day Tuesday enrolled and she came through the vice-principal's office wearing those gloves. The vice-principal said, 'You don't wear gloves to school.' Tuesday's reply was, 'I'm a lady and ladies wear gloves, so I'm going to wear my gloves to school.' " On another occasion, when a teacher chastised her for being absent from class, Tuesday said something like, "Listen, when I'm a big star you'll still be here making peanuts."

For entirely different reasons, Barbara Parkins and Yvette Mimieux—also members of the class of 1961—were likewise disgruntled with their high school alma mater. Born in Vancouver, Parkins was an accomplished dancer by the time she and her mother moved to Los Angeles in the late Fifties. The Canadian schools she had attended must have differed considerably from the cliquish, style-conscious atmosphere of Hollywood High, for young Barbara was quite unhappy at her new school. A self-professed loner, she found Hollywood High oppressively social-minded. After school she attended a dance class, and it was at one of her recitals that she was discovered by an MCA talent agent who booked her for a small part on *Wagon Train*. It must have been with some surprise that her classmates saw shy, insecure Barbara metamorphose into Betty Anderson, the bold little strumpet she played with such verve on *Peyton Place*.

Yvette Mimieux found the high school experience claustrophobic and petty. "I hated it," she told her studio publicist. "Classrooms are prisons. I was less well-dressed than others in my class, everything I did was wrong. I felt different, said off-beat things, and was frequently held up to ridicule and criticism by kids who felt any evidence of originality was a drawback." John Ingle remembers her as a "talented youngster with good looks you couldn't help but notice." Says Willard Hansen: "She was certainly not the typical bobby-soxer, sort of a loner."

Mimieux had grown up in Hollywood and had, like young Taffy Paul, become blasé about the so-called glamour of the film industry. Thus, as a student at Hollywood High, she was more interested in art than acting (science and the arts was her major) and aspired to a career as a fashion designer and possibly later as a serious artist. If, as she claims, she was "held up to ridicule," the barbs probably did not emanate from the school's male contingent. Yvette, who had been a professional model since the age of fourteen, was one of the best-looking girls on campus. Throughout her high school career she held a number of local beauty queen titles, including Miss Harbor Day of 1957, National Electric Week Queen of 1959, Los Angeles Boat Show Queen of 1958, and Los Angeles Art Directors Queen of 1958.

If the story is to be believed, Yvette Mimieux's big break literally fell out of the sky one sunny afternoon. The much-publicized event occurred in Griffith Park when she was fifteen years old. Supposedly, she had been out horseback riding when a helicopter got caught in an updraft and was forced to make an emergency landing not far from where she was riding. As luck would have it, the pilot was James Bryon, one of Hollywood's most powerful press agents, on his way to photograph a dragracing event. Pulling himself out of the chopper, he took one look at the gorgeous teenager astride the horse and saw the makings of a star. Two weeks later Yvette found herself cutting a class at Hollywood High to have lunch with Bryon at the famous Brown Derby restaurant, whereupon he signed her to a managerial contract. Many of her Hollywood High schoolmates would see beautiful Yvette on the big screen a few years later, in the popular teen hit *Where the Boys Are*. But real fame came some years later when she played a bikinied surfer with a crippling disease on the top-rated *Dr. Kildare* TV series.

3.

Sex is not the only subject dealt with in books. Contrary to popular belief, *The Carpetbaggers* and *Tropic of Cancer* are not the only kind of books on the shelves.

—From an editorial
in *The News*, 1964

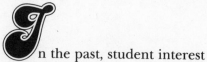n the past, student interest in moviemaking had been generally limited to drab documentary depictions of school ceremonies and athletic events, but by the early Sixties Hollywood High's aspiring filmmakers decided to take a shot at making a commercial motion picture. In 1962 a group of students got together and, under the auspices of Desilu Studios, wrote, produced, and directed a movie. The idea behind the project was primarily to gain experience in film production, but a few of the more optimistic participants had far loftier fantasies. "When the movie is completed," one of them confidently told the school paper, "we plan to sell it to one of the studios." The studios politely passed.

The following year, eleven students got together on Saturdays to collaborate on writing an episode of *Dr. Kildare.* According to *The News*, its subject was the "fight game," and the completed script would be sent to the producers of the show. The school paper never mentioned the project again.

Students whose interests lay beyond the film industry had a host of newly formed clubs to choose from. The medical club, established in 1961, heard speeches given by doctors and dentists, performed volunteer work at local hospitals, and, in 1963, adopted an entire Vietnamese village, providing its inhabitants with medicine, soap, and toys. The popular folk song club, first proposed in the late Fifties, held its first hootenanny in a student assembly in November 1963. Enrollment in the debate club—which had fallen in the recent past—rose markedly in the early Sixties, as more and more students were inspired by the speechifying skills of President John F. Kennedy. Kennedy's influence also led to increased interest in physical fitness, speed-reading, and school politics, and more than a few Hollywood High students sported a "Kennedy haircut" (while the school's fashion-conscious girls emulated Jackie Kennedy's look).

Meanwhile, in spite of principal Perry's emergency measures, the campus population had swelled to twenty-four hundred boys and girls. A new principal—Dr. Charles E. Sutcliffe—was hired in 1962, and during his first semester all Hollywood High students were programmed through electronic data processing for the first time. Since so many students now drove to school, one of the more pressing dilemmas resulting from the population explosion was a severe shortage of parking on or near the campus. Students complained that the lack of parking facilities made it necessary for them to arrive some forty-five minutes early in order to find a space. "It took longer to find a parking space than it did to get to school," recalls one car-burdened alumnus. The situation was only somewhat relieved when, after a heated debate, the administration decided to turn the school's front lawn into a faculty parking lot. The grassy knoll where

Fay Wray and many others had once eaten their bag lunches amid the fragrant poinsettias was now a paved-over blacktop drive.

But campus life was changing in other, more significant ways. "Has Beatlemania Hit Hollywood High?" the school newspaper asked on April 10, 1964, a short two months after the British rockers debuted on the *Ed Sullivan Show*. The answer was clearly yes. By this time, a number of Hollywood High's male students had already taken to emulating the group's hairstyle, a trend that the typically conservative, somewhat straitlaced editors of the school paper dismissed as a "passing fad." "Certain students sporting shaggy Beatle wigs can be seen if you care to look," the editors observed. "You may happen to want to comment about those strange haircuts. Well don't; they aren't really strange; they just date back to the 15th Century (A.D.!). You may ask why the girls of America actually scream and rave about these boys. Well, no one can answer that except the girls that scream and rave. Certainly, the Beatles must have a charm. What it is, is only evident to their fans, not to the people who sit disgustedly wondering."

Much to the chagrin of the student editorial board, as well as of the administration, the so-called passing fad would turn out to be a protracted one. In the fall of 1964, with the Rolling Stones and the Dave Clark Five joining the Beatles as campus favorites, the Girls League came out against long hair in its official code of dress, a strict set of rules that outlawed hats and required that the boys tuck in their shirts and leave all but the top buttons fastened. The administration did its best to enforce the dress code, but with twenty-four hundred students roaming the campus, the shirttail situation was virtually unmanageable.

Music dominated the campus as never before. Each new Beatle album was eagerly awaited, and in 1965, Hollywood High started its own radio station. That year the big songs were "Gloria," "Stop in the Name of Love," "Mrs. Brown (You've Got a Lovely Daughter)," and "Ticket to Ride." New words like *groovy* and *psychedelic* entered the campus argot, and an article on yoga appeared in the school paper. Eternally reactionary, the student editors continued to decry the new wave: "Many people share the belief that to be an individualist one must wear strange clothes, have an even stranger haircut, talk with words not found in Webster's, and play the guitar. Is that what Hollywood High students believe?"

4.

Student Council is a learning experience. Teenagers learn how to work and communicate more
effectively with their peers as well as with adults.

—John Ritter (class of '66)

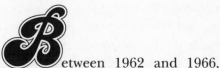etween 1962 and 1966,
just before the counterculture enveloped the campus,
Hollywood High graduated a healthy crop of student talent which included four well-known actresses, two actors,
two classical pianists, and one ballet star.

The first of this illustrious group was Swoosie Kurtz,
who received her diploma with the class of 1962. Born
in Omaha, Nebraska, Swoosie is the daughter of noted
World War II pilot Frank Kurtz, who graduated from
Hollywood High with the class of 1930. She was named
after her father's celebrated B-17 bomber, *The Swoose*,
which was constructed from the wreckage of a number
of other planes, all destroyed when the Japanese bombed
an airfield in Manila early on in the war. The jerry-built
Swoose got its peculiar nickname from its insignia—an
odd-looking creature that was half swan and half goose.

Young Swoosie Kurtz's high school career had its ups
and downs. She ran for the student council three times,
but never won a seat; she tried out for the pom-pom
squad, but didn't make it. Her successes were in academics and drama. After playing a small role in the 1961

spring production, *Our Town*, she was given a much big-ger part in the fall play, *The Skin of Our Teeth*. Her acting ability was honored her senior year, when she was one of several students chosen to perform at the annual Shakespeare Festival at UCLA, where she played Hermia in *A Midsummer Night's Dream*, described by John Ingle as "a knockout production—one of the best." An honor roll student for much of her high school tenure, Swoosie Kurtz received the distinguished "gold seal diploma" at graduation. "She was a dynamite talent," says John Ingle, "and a pleasure to work with." Today Ingle and his for-mer student maintain a close friendship.

Meredith Baxter Birney and Johnny Crawford were juniors the year after Swoosie Kurtz graduated. Crawford had been a child star, starting as an extra in a Loretta Young flick at the age of three. Later he was a Mouse-keteer on Walt Disney's *Mickey Mouse Club,* but he is best remembered for his role as Chuck Connors's son in the popular *Rifleman* TV series. In 1963, shortly after *Rifle-man* was canceled, Crawford entered Hollywood High, where he majored in French and sang in the glee club. The boy who sat next to him at choir practice was Mike Smith, another ex-Mouseketeer.

Meredith Baxter Birney (then known simply as Mere-dith Baxter) also had a show business background. Her father was radio announcer Tom Baxter, and her mother, actress Whitney Blake, had played Missy on the television series *Hazel*. By her own account, young Meredith Baxter was a shy, quiet teenager who had difficulty making friends and spent a good deal of her time alone, reading. She sang in the girls' glee club and participated in sev-eral school productions, including the 1963 fall play, *An-*

tigone (she was part of the chorus), and during her senior year, *The Tempest* (she played Iris). Most of her few close friends were other members of the school's drama group. "I was never Miss Popularity," she recalled for the *Ladies' Home Journal* in 1986. "I couldn't get into the social clubs when I wanted to and by the time they got around to me, I wasn't interested. I used to stand in front of my class and say, 'My mom's on TV tonight,' as if that would garner me some friends or attention that I wasn't getting otherwise. I was a jerk." Today's students at Hollywood High know Meredith Baxter Birney as the mother on TV's *Family Ties*.

Unlike Meredith Baxter, Barbara Hershey (class of 1965) had no family ties to show business. (Her father wrote the sweeps column for the *Racing Form*.) A native of Hollywood, she was born Barbara Herzstein, and as far back as she can remember, she was possessed of only one goal. "Whenever anyone asked me what I wanted to be when I grew up, I always answered 'an actress,'" she told a studio publicist. "As soon as I could talk, I'd go to the movies and then come home and act out the various parts. My family called me Sarah Bernhardt."

Though student dramatics would soon consume most of her energies, young Barbara Herzstein spent the first half of her sophomore year acting out the role of the typical Hollywood High coed. She joined the girls' drill team and was initiated into the Thetas, an honor accorded only the prettiest campus coeds. Throughout her tenure at the school, she earned mostly A's and B's, though she claims not to have been overly interested in any of her subjects other than drama. "I was a responsible student," she recalls. "I didn't shirk, though I wasn't

Barbara Hershey (left) played one of the Lovers in Hollywood High's 1965 production of *The Madwoman of Chaillot.*

fascinated by school. I was conscientious, but not studious. I was the one who always did extra reports."

She was also, as she recalls, "very shy and very naive.
I was a good girl and never ever got into any trouble,
never ditched class or cut assembly." She dated a few
boys during her sophomore year, and later went steady
with a guitar player who had his own band. ("I remember
standing around at parties while he played.") One year
she had a crush on the student body president, who took
her to a prom and promptly abandoned her to "chat
with his buddies," and "I remember my heart thumping
whenever I saw Johnny Crawford on campus." English
and science were her favorite subjects, while math and
history made her cringe.

Halfway through her sophomore year, Barbara Hershey quit the drill team and the girls' club and enrolled
in John Ingle's drama class. From that point on, her dedication to student theatre became almost obsessive, and
those who remember her say that she appeared to be "in
a world of her own."

"Drama removed me from some of the classic high
school activities," Barbara claims. "It was something I was
deeply passionate about, and it was almost as if I had
blinders on. I just wasn't real conscious of what was going on around me, other than in the drama department.
Kids could've been shooting up in the halls and I
wouldn't have noticed."

John Ingle had a profound effect on her: "He was a
great drama teacher," Barbara recollects. "He was almost
like a preacher in that he had a reverence for acting. You
couldn't help but catch the fever from him. He was the
first person who introduced acting to me in a serious,

workaholic kind of way." Within a short period of time, she became one of Ingle's favorites. "I adored her," he says. "She was a rebel all right, but a productive, creative, and very talented rebel." Bashful and soft-spoken off-stage, Barbara Herzstein must have come alive under the spotlight, for she was continually given the quirkiest roles. Her high school acting resume is quite a remarkable one. She played Lady Macbeth one year, the acerbic Martha in *Who's Afraid of Virginia Woolf?* the next, and was featured as Irma in *The Madwoman of Chaillot* in autumn of 1964. "I chose the nuttiest parts," she later confessed, "because I knew I'd be an ingenue for a long time."

As it turned out, she was one of the last ingenues to be discovered while still attending Hollywood High. It happened in the middle of her senior year. A talent agent, looking for experienced young actresses, called the school's drama department for recommendations. Barbara's name was mentioned and she was sent to the agent's office to give a reading. "I read a scene from *The Rainmaker*," she recalled. "The agent signed me the same day and started me on the audition rounds." (Since she had not yet graduated, she took a leave from Hollywood High and later completed her last semester at Fairfax High's summer school.) After some fifty interviews, she got her first job: a small role opposite Sally Field in the TV series *Gidget*, but it was a start. She made her first film, *With Six You Get Eggroll*, two years later. "I didn't really learn that much about acting at Hollywood High," she reflected years after leaving the school. "But I did learn a lot about having nerve and dealing with the pain of rejection."

For some reason Hollywood High produced three of

265

its most prominent classical artists during the Sixties. Pianist Gerald Robbins (class of 1963) was accompanist to the school's glee clubs and choirs before soloing with the Los Angeles Philharmonic his junior year. In May 1962 he performed *Rhapsody in Blue* at Hollywood High's spring concert.

Following Robbins's graduation, another young musical prodigy entered Hollywood High. Horacio Gutierez had immigrated to Los Angeles from Cuba in 1961 and had studied the piano for most of his life when he registered as a science major with the class of 1966. *The News* featured him in a front-page article when, during his senior year, he performed in a "Young Peoples' Concert" with Leonard Bernstein and the New York Philharmonic. "Horacio wishes to continue his piano playing after graduation and would like to be a concert pianist," the paper declared. In fact, he played his piano *during* graduation, for he was the featured soloist at Hollywood High's 1966 commencement ceremony.

Dancer-choreographer John Clifford went through Hollywood High with the class of 1965, but doesn't seem to have found much inspiration in the experience. "I didn't give a damn for school," he recollected. "It was a bore. If you have some interest in art, schools don't teach you a thing. I was an honors student when I wasn't choreographing or directing a musical. The rest of the time, my studies were erratic." Clifford majored in music and art, and played the role of Ariel in *The Tempest,* the same production that featured Meredith Baxter in the lesser role of Iris. After graduation, he became a "Hollywood gypsy," dancing and acting on episodes of various television series, including *The Donna Reed Show* and *Death*

Valley Days. He then moved to New York to study ballet. Within a few years he was a dancer and choreographer with the New York City Ballet and, later, founder and director of the Los Angeles Ballet.

John Ritter was a junior when Clifford graduated in 1965. Born in Burbank, the son of Western star Tex Ritter, young John made a smashing success of his high school career. "It was one of the happiest periods of my life," he recalls. "I was on fire in those days. I remember waking up each morning just raring to go."

An excellent student with a grade point average well above the 3.0 level, he was elected vice-president of the junior class in 1965 and student body president the following year. For the latter office, he ran unopposed, an unprecedented distinction. "I had a pretty big political machine going by then," he says. "I was kind of a Boss Tweedledee. I ran on the ticket that we could have fun and also get things done." Like many youngsters, Ritter had been strongly influenced by John F. Kennedy. "I had two goals in high school. I wanted to be a Democratic senator from California and play first base for the Dodgers, kind of Sixties version of Steve Garvey, you might say."

While a smattering of the boys on campus were beginning to sport longish hair and faded blue jeans, Ritter maintained a clean-cut appearance, which he remembers as "a kind of surfer–Dobie Gillis look." "He was the type that wore white Levi's, madras shirts, and Hush Puppies," recalls one of Ritter's schoolmates. "He was a real clean-cut boy, with quite a sense of humor. He didn't fall down and bump into walls, but he did make clever remarks during class."

Student Council President John Ritter makes a point while two ador-
ing coeds look on. Ritter was so popular, he ran unopposed for the
office.

That is not to say that Ritter was a straight arrow. Far from it. "I might have looked conservative and straight, but I had a hippie sense of humor. I was the Number One Class Clown. At dances, which were wild in those days, I was the guy who made wisecracks and goofed around. I was irreverent. In fact, I almost got thrown out of school in 1965 for defending a girl who was reading *Candy,* which was taboo in those days. One of the more conservative coaches had it in for me." The only real hippies Ritter recalls seeing in those days were in the drama department, but the subject of nonconformity was clearly on the minds of the school's straitlaced newspaper editors. In response to a 1965 newspaper poll surveying student attitudes toward "weirdness and individualism," Ritter showed himself possessed of a politician's ability not to alienate anyone. "One who does not adhere to the social and ethical standards of his group is an individualist, I guess," is the deft quote that ran under his name.

Throughout his high school career, Ritter was highly popular and widely respected, among both teachers and students, for his wit and intelligence. Hollywood High's cliquishness did not put him off. "I made it a point to be friends with everybody. I was a kind of Zelig—I'd immediately take on the personality traits of the people I was hanging around with." English was his best subject, and he particularly remembers being inspired by honors English teacher Harry Major. "I wasn't too hot in math or anything else that had to do with numbers," he claims. "At one point I was thinking of getting an accountant and taking him to class with me."

The tremendous popularity Ritter enjoyed in high school is evidenced in the pages of the school newspaper. Following his election as student body president, *The News* was effusive: "John will be one of the most active, wittiest presidents Hollywood High has ever seen," one article proclaimed. "With John Ritter guiding, we should have a promising semester," another predicted. "John is a cool, witty, smart, sophisticated, suave student," sang yet another. Clad in jacket and tie, his hair short and well groomed, young Ritter announced an ambitious platform of innovations he hoped to carry out during his term of office. Among his primary goals: more diversified assemblies, movies in the auditorium during lunchtime to ease the overcrowding on the quad, greater publicity for school events, and celebrity award ceremonies. "His new ideas and activities will keep the student council constantly busy," the school newspaper observed. According to Ritter, every single one of his promises was fulfilled. "We even invented a new dance called the Sheik Shake, and painted all the campus trash cans red and white."

Though student government kept him busy, John Ritter was no slouch in the dating department. During his junior and senior years, he had a steady—a girl who attended a nearby Catholic school. Monogamy, however, did not make him immune from the usual teenage crushes, and one in particular stands out in his mind, even today. "I had a major crush on Barbara Hershey," he confesses. "She was a wonderful actress and I used to love to watch her perform. Unfortunately, she was a class ahead of me and had a boyfriend, who I hoped would have a severe accident and leave the field open to me, but it was all just a teenage fantasy, of course. In the end, I was loyal to my girl."

The suave, sophisticated Ritter did have at least one embarrassing moment in high school. Ritter has never forgotten his first encounter with piano prodigy class-mate Horacio Gutierez: "I was entertaining some girls at a party, playing 'Chopsticks' on the piano, rather pathet-ically as I recall. Horacio, whom I did not know at the time, came over and asked me to show him how to play it. I gave him a quick lesson and then he sat down and proceeded to run through some incredibly complex Mo-zart piece. He was a prodigy, and here I thought I was going to teach him a few tricks."

John Ritter was one of Hollywood High's few illustri-ous alumni to be elected an Ephebian ("I was damned proud of that"), an honor bestowed on those graduating students who demonstrate outstanding character, schol-arship, and leadership during their high school careers. It was the sort of honor a budding John F. Kennedy would have cherished. But as a college freshman the fol-lowing year, Ritter would give up his political aspirations ("Robert Kennedy's assassination just took the wind out of my sails") and take an active interest in drama, a sub-ject he had showed little interest in at Hollywood High.

5.

Appropriate dress for school does not include mini-skirts.

—From *The News*, 1966

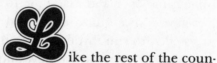ike the rest of the country, Hollywood High was experiencing a new political consciousness, ushered in by what the school newspaper disparagingly referred to as *weirdoes* (the term *hippies* had not come into wide use yet). "Though there have always been a percentage of politically-minded teenagers," *The News* noted, "the great majority have never really responded. This pattern is rapidly changing." Protest demonstrations at the nearby University of California at Berkeley, the Vietnam War, and the civil rights movement were all hotly debated topics the year John Ritter graduated, and there was little consensus about them among the students, as a schoolwide poll, conducted early in 1966, vividly illustrates. Though sixty-two percent of the students thought protest demonstrations were nothing more than a fad, fifty percent claimed to have been in agreement with the protesters at least part of the time. In answer to the query "What is the greatest challenge facing the U.S today?" the students were evenly divided between Vietnam and civil rights. As for the outcome of the Vietnam War, thirty-eight percent predicted it

would end in stalemate, three percent thought the United States would lose, and only thirty percent of the students saw an American victory in the offing (the remainder were undecided). But by the following year, more than a few Hollywood High students were becoming actively involved in demonstrations, including a "love-in" held at Griffith Park and a huge antiwar protest march through the streets of Hollywood in June 1967.

Since World War I, Hollywood High had always held its award-winning ROTC battalion in high esteem, but by 1968 the students were divided on whether or not the school should sanction military training. Pro and con arguments appeared in the school paper, and scattered episodes of heckling occurred when the uniformed trainees went out to drill. Other debates that raged that year concerned the legalization of marijuana and the advisability of altering Hollywood High's grading system from the numerical to the pass/fail method. Marijuana smoking was common on campus in the late Sixties—students would score a *joint* or a *lid* on the front lawn during lunchtime and smoke in the athletics field's bleachers or in their cars between classes. Expulsion was the penalty for being caught smoking or *holding*, but by the late Sixties the administration found pot use difficult to control, and there is no mention of widespread expulsion in the pages of *The News*.

Much to the chagrin of the administration, growing numbers of students were demonstrating an affinity for a wide variety of unusual attire, none of which conformed to the school's concept of conventional dress. The era's fashions—bell-bottom blue jeans, tie-dyed T-shirts, Frye boots, miniskirts, and all manner of hairstyles—

made dress code enforcement more than a little prob-
lematical, but the administration managed to persevere.
As Hollywood High's current drama director, Jerry Melton, recalls: "When I came to Hollywood High in 1968,
Hollywood Boulevard was awash with hippies, but the
campus was still clean-cut, like something out of the past.
The administration held on to the dress code as long as
it could, practically took it to the courts."

If the administration stuck to traditional conserva-
tism, the school newspaper, long a stronghold of the
school's stodgier constituency, soon gave way to liberalized attitudes. In 1967 its editors cited the example of
Antioch College to *support* the argument that Hollywood
High adopt a pass/fail system of grading. "A good feature
of Antioch is that the students are not given grades," the
paper explained. "Instead, the instructor prepares a sum-
mary stating whether the student has earned credit." But
Hollywood High was a high school, not a private college,
and the administration stuck to the old-fashioned grade
point system, at least for the time being. It would not be
until the early Seventies that an experimental study program—called The Alternative School—would find a
home on campus.

But the most heated debate—the one that pitted the
students firmly against the administration—involved the
issue of the Student Bill of Rights. Late in the Sixties,
students representing most of the schools in the Los Angeles high school district got together and produced a
document that accorded them certain rights. Among
these was the right of free discussion of any issue at
school, freedom from "unreasonable search and sei-
zure," and the right to petition the administration for

change. The students wanted their respective schools to adopt the document, but Hollywood High's administration firmly rejected it.

Early in 1970 tensions erupted at Hollywood High when four candidates for the student council claimed that they had been denied their right of free discussion. They charged that the administration of the school had censored certain passages from their campaign speeches. They had not been permitted, they claimed, to mention the Black Panthers, the police, or the draft. References to the school dress code and the Student Bill of Rights had also been excised. A rally to inform the student body of this tyranny was held on the school lawn facing Sunset Boulevard, and a sit-down protest erupted in front of the vice-principal's office. But the administration did not give in. The rally was dispersed and eight of its leaders were suspended. Hollywood High was not Berkeley. But Hollywood High wasn't what it used to be. And neither, for that matter, was Hollywood.

6.

Vandalism on campus is becoming increasingly evident.

—From an editorial
in *The News*, 1969

y the late Sixties, the city
of Hollywood was hopelessly mired in a progressive state
of deterioration. The affluent middle-class families who
had once populated the flatlands had been moving out
steadily, replaced by an ever-expanding influx of poor,
often uneducated, and non-English-speaking immigrants,
mostly Hispanics, Asians, and Armenians. Rents were going down and many of the area's high-class stores were
forced out of business. Meanwhile, liberalized obscenity
laws had resulted in the opening of a number of porno
shops and X-rated theatres on Hollywood Boulevard.
Ironically, many of the latter took residence in buildings
that had formerly housed art film theatres. The Vista,
which had once specialized in Russian film classics, was
now a gay movie theatre. And before it became a porn
house, the theatre that is now known as The Pussycat had
run Bresson's *Diary of a Country Priest*.

But many Hollywoodians blame the youth movement
of the Sixties for the rapid decay of their city. Indeed, of
all the communities that make up Los Angeles, it was
Hollywood that felt the counterculture's impact the most.

By 1967 the streets of the city were awash with the un-washed from every corner of the country. Hippies, many of them without money, food, or a place to sleep, poured in from everywhere, lured by the movie capital's glittery reputation. Discos and coffee shops like the Whiskey A Go-Go and The Trip opened in buildings that had once housed Hollywood's lavish nightclubs. Record stores and head shops sprang up all along Hollywood Boulevard, nestled between the massage parlors and adult book-stores. Light shows and rock concerts were held at Grif-fith Park. The streets were alive with surfers, Hell's Angels, and hippies, many of whom made drug deals on the street in broad daylight. Vandalism, vagrancy, pan-handling, and prostitution were on the rise.

Reacting to the complaints of its citizens, Holly-wood's city council passed a number of ordinances de-signed to curb the excesses of the growing street scene. A ten P.M. curfew was enacted and loitering laws were passed, but none of these ordinances came close to solv-ing the city's problems. Hollywood was completely over-taken, and the only option left to its more respectable citizens was to escape.

By the late Sixties, Hollywood High began to feel the effects of the community's deterioration. For one thing, the surrounding neighborhood was now filled with mas-sage parlors, adult bookstores, and porn theatres, hardly a wholesome environment for a school. Vandalism had spread from the streets to the campus, and the school newspaper complained bitterly of repeated incidents of smashed classroom windows and trash cans set on fire. Cutting classes was becoming an epidemic, and the graf-fiti problem was out of control. Drug use was proliferating. Moreover, the texture of the student body was changing. Some middle-class Hollywoodians who remained in the city were taking their children out of Hollywood High and sending them to private schools in other parts of Los Angeles. More and more, these students were being replaced by non-English-speaking children from Asia and Latin America.

As if all of that weren't enough, Hollywood High was dealt what many consider to have been a fatal blow in 1968. Concerned with overcrowding and the problem of transporting students over long distances, the Los Angeles school board decided that year to drastically shrink the Hollywood district boundaries. As a result, upper-middle-class areas like Toluca Lake and Studio City, which had once sent their young people to Hollywood High, were suddenly located in another school district. "That was the turning point," observed Hollywood High English teacher Harry Major in the pages of *The News*. "In one blow, we lost the cream of our students."

PART SEVEN

The Blackboard Jungle

1970-1986

1.

Like a deadly cancer, campus violence is becoming more and more frequent.
—From the school newspaper, 1976

*T*he decline of Hollywood and its venerable old high school continued at an even greater pace throughout the first half of the new decade. Hollywood Boulevard was fast becoming Los Angeles's answer to Times Square, a seedy area populated by derelicts, hookers, and Hell's Angels, many of whom congregated near the Hollywood High campus. Even the most stalwart Hollywoodians were giving up on their city and moving to the Valley, where new high schools were springing up to accommodate the school board's redistricting plan. As Harry Major had predicted, Hollywood High was losing its best students. And many of their replacements did not even speak English.

As all these demographic changes in the school were taking place, Hollywood High found itself woefully unprepared to deal with the results. Everything was simply happening too fast. Until 1968, English had been the native language of ninety-eight percent of the student body, but that figure was rapidly eroding, and with it went the school's academic standing. Vandalism was getting out of hand. Narcotics arrests were rising. Street people were wandering freely on and off the campus. Muggings and campus violence, which were generally isolated events in the late Sixties, were increasing in frequency, and by 1974 a studentwide poll revealed violence on campus as the major problem affecting the school.

Pregnancy among high school girls was also on the rise (the Los Angeles area reported ten thousand such pregnancies in 1970), and venereal disease was spreading at an alarming enough rate for the school paper to publish an editorial entitled "Stop VD Plague." "Part of the reason for soaring teenage birth rates may be society's newly cultivated hang-loose attitude toward sex," the paper concluded. Counseling services were set up, but the debate over sex education continued. Students in favor of adding regular sex education to the curriculum argued that most parents were too embarrassed to discuss the subject with their children; the opposition held that sex education belonged in the home. The conflict was partially resolved in early 1973, when Hollywood High finally added sex education to its health classes, though parental permission was required by state law.

Apathy among the student body had also become a problem. Absenteeism was flagrant, and many students complained that the required assemblies (nicknamed *auds*) had become boring and irrelevant. "Lots of students find school boring," the newspaper groused. "Perhaps the majority of students find it boring, but instead of making the best of it, they are captured in the great ho-hum." School spirit was lacking, membership in school activities was low, and even attendance at football games was sparse. "People used to snicker at the drill teams and cheerleaders," says one member of the class of 1974.

The administration of Hollywood High—which changed leadership four times in five years during the Seventies—attempted to confront the school's many problems with a curious mixture of commonsense capitulation, firm resolve, and an occasional arbitrary strictness that still fell short of being effective. The dress code, which the administration had staunchly upheld throughout the Sixties, was revised—girls were now allowed to wear pantsuits and slacks to school; boys with parental approval could let their hair grow, provided it remained "above the bottom of the shirt collar." In 1974 coeds were allowed to participate in all boys' sports except those involving contact. To respond to students' demands for a place to smoke, the athletics field bleachers were designated as a student smoking area, but marijuana smokers soon abused that privilege. With violence on the rise, the administration took several stern measures: Security guards and members of the faculty were instructed to comb the campus during free periods in search of outbreaks, and students desirous of leaving classes, even for something as trivial as a glass of water or a trip to the bathroom, were required to carry a pass signed by the teacher. That may have helped curb violence by students, but was ineffective against incursions from the increasingly seedy neighborhood just beyond. Talk of erecting a high fence around the campus as a means of preventing violence began in 1976, and as a more immediate response, the girls were taught self-defense techniques in gym class.

283

The school may have had its problems, many of them severe, but the more motivated students on campus—and there still were some—managed to keep a faint glimmer of the old spirit alive. When the school ran a deficit in 1970, students raised funds by selling tins of toffee-covered peanuts for a dollar apiece in what was called "The P'Nuttle Campaign." That same year, the students organized Hollywood High's first Holly-Olympics, a campuswide event featuring such activities as a tug of war, an egg toss, and a chariot race. The faculty was invited to participate. A group of art students, outraged by the proliferation of graffiti, began covering the walls with colorful murals, many of which still exist unmarred. And in 1974, to help once again with the school's deficit, students organized a Walk-a-Thon. That same year, an event called Donkey Basketball, in which faculty members played the game on real live mules, proved a big success.

Students were not entirely indifferent to the world around them either. In response to the intellectual and sociological trends of the day, a lively debate on women's liberation gripped the campus in the early Seventies—with the boys coming out heavily in favor of girls asking boys on dates. Bowing to popular demand, the library began subscribing to *Ms. Magazine, The Mother Earth News,* and *Sierra,* and astrology, transcendental meditation, ecology, and health food were all much discussed.

The student body also maintained its long-standing interest in show business with the school administration doing what it could to perpetuate Hollywood High's unique connection to the motion picture industry. A course in television and motion picture arts and sciences was initiated in 1970 (it was taught by William Gass, a

former talent agent), and students continued to demonstrate an active interest in all aspects of filmmaking.
School productions continued on schedule, and by most
accounts, their professionalism had not deteriorated.
Nevertheless, a slight degree of cynicism regarding the
film industry and Hollywood High's long relationship to
it seemed to have set in. Hollywood High graduates were
no longer rushing off in droves to the studios as so many
of their predecessors had. By the mid-Seventies, most recent alumni were clerk-typists, salespeople, factory workers, or stenographers, according to a campus poll. In a
newspaper article entitled "Don't Get Tinsel Up Your
Nose," one particularly cynical student cast a jaundiced
eye on the appeal and promise of Hollywood stardom:
"For a city, Hollywood is okay, but who cares about the
glamour of show business? Does anyone notice stars on
Hollywood Boulevard? Only tourists visit Grauman's Chinese to look at stars' footprints. I bet there are some
mighty old ladies still sipping malteds in their sojourn of
discovery, a million talents milked dry by that putrid
promise, 'Baby, I'm gonna make you a star.'"

2.

I don't want much really, just Elton John and the Los Angeles Rams.

> —Charlene Tilton's response
> to a student poll on
> Christmas wishes, 1975

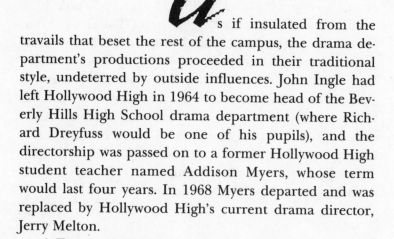s if insulated from the travails that beset the rest of the campus, the drama department's productions proceeded in their traditional style, undeterred by outside influences. John Ingle had left Hollywood High in 1964 to become head of the Beverly Hills High School drama department (where Richard Dreyfuss would be one of his pupils), and the directorship was passed on to a former Hollywood High student teacher named Addison Myers, whose term would last four years. In 1968 Myers departed and was replaced by Hollywood High's current drama director, Jerry Melton.

A Texan, Melton was educated at North Texas State University, Cal State Northridge, and UCLA. His family represents a virtual Hollywood High dynasty. His wife, Ruthe, attended the school, class of 1949, and was a featured player in Arthur Kachel's 1948 production of *H.M.S. Pinafore*; her parents graduated from Hollywood High in the late Twenties; and Melton's three children are all Hollywood High alumni. Though Jerry Melton took up the reins of the drama department at the very outset of Hollywood High's decline, he asserts that the level of discipline and diligence among the school's thespians showed no signs of deterioration.

The last major on-campus discovery of record had taken place during Addison Myers's tenure in 1966, when a student named Hilarie Thompson was offered a long-term contract by Screen Gems as a result of her performance in Hollywood High's production of *My Fair Lady*. (The play costarred former child star Evelyn Rudie in the role of Henry Higgins's mother.) After 1966, the output of student talent would be reduced to a trickle.

That trickle did, however, include Robert Carradine and Diana Canova, who attended the school in the early Seventies, when Hollywood High was still holding on to a semblance of its former reputation. "Those were the days before Hollywood High was fenced in," Robert Carradine recalls, "and we'd hang out on the front lawn every day at lunchtime. The pretty girls—and there were plenty of them then—used to love to hang out there because they'd get honks from all the passing cars. It was like theatre on the lawn every lunch hour."

Bobby Carradine, youngest son of actor John Carradine, had received most of his education at a nearby private boarding school, and when he registered at Hollywood High in 1970, the hippie era was in full flower. By his own description, Carradine looked the part to the hilt: "I used to come to school in these weird get-ups," he recollects. "My favorite outfit consisted of a pair of burgundy cutoffs, Frye boots, a goatskin shirt that was so roughly tanned it looked like shit was hanging off it, and an orange cape with a white satin lining. My hair was down to the middle of my back, and my sideburns were so long they were almost muttonchops. I suppose I was trying to make some kind of statement or something." At the time, Bobby's brother David was living in Laurel Canyon with another former Hollywood High student, Barbara Hershey, and during his two-year tenure at the school, Bobby occupied their small guest house. "I was into horticulture in those days," he confesses. "I grew some very potent pot, which I called 'Laurel Canyon Purple,' your basic one-hit grass."

Bobby Carradine's record at Hollywood High was, as he tells it, mixed at best. He managed to maintain a C average, with a sprinkling of B's in English and music appreciation—depending on how much he liked the teacher—and straight A's in metal shop, his favorite course. Metal shop appealed to him because he was interested in motorcycles and cars at the time, and one of his fondest memories of Hollywood High was constructing a pair of headers for his car—a rare English racing model called a Turner. "I had two periods of metal shop in a row," Carradine recalls. "It was definitely the high point for me at Hollywood High." Another high point was soccer. Carradine played on Hollywood High's very first soccer team. "Because of all the Latin students on campus, we had plenty of soccer talent. There were only two North American players on the team, and I was one of them." He ended up winning a varsity letter in the sport and regrets to this day that he never bothered to buy a Hollywood High letter sweater to display it on (though it probably would have clashed with the goatskin shirt and cape).

Carradine's record with Hollywood High's reputable drama department did not match his achievements on the soccer field or in metal shop. Jerry Melton remembers him as "a real laid-back kind of hippie. I failed him in play production—all he was interested in while he was at Hollywood High was sitting around and playing the guitar. I think he was in one play, but he didn't have a speaking role." Actually, Carradine remembers being in two plays: a student-directed production of *Spoon River Anthology* and *The Admirable Crichton*. "I had one line in *Crichton*," he says. "I walked out on stage and said, 'Yes, sir.' That was it. Believe it or not, I made my whole family come and see it."

In the early Seventies, Hollywood High was still very cliquish, and Carradine often found himself on the outside looking in. "I didn't really belong. For some reason, I couldn't seem to infiltrate any of the high school cliques. There were the good-looking guys, who all hung out together, but I couldn't get into that group. There were the studious types, but I didn't belong with them either. I ended up with the musicians and pot smokers." He also recalls dating two or three girls on a more or less steady basis, and having a crush on one of the cheerleaders. "I think I actually managed to take her out once," he says tentatively, "but it didn't go anywhere."

Bobby Carradine did not attend his graduation ceremonies, for in 1971 he was plucked out of school to play opposite John Wayne in *The Cowboys*. Carradine's film debut did not escape the notice of the student body. In an interview in *The News*, Carradine downplayed the importance of his famous name: "Getting the part of Slim Honeycutt in the movie had nothing to do with being a member of the Carradine family," he claimed. "I was among eight hundred kids interviewed for the part." Today's Hollywood High students know him as the star of the teen film *Revenge of the Nerds.*

Though they were classmates, Bobby Carradine and Diana Canova did not know each other while at Hollywood High. Having been brought up in Hollywood from the age of three, the daughter of comedienne Judy Canova, young Diana Canova had always wanted to be an actress. Music, dancing, and singing were her schooltime passions, but her Hollywood High career seems to have been a lonely one. Described by her classmates as "sweet but fat," Diana (known on campus as Dee Dee) was a bit of a loner. "I was always an outsider because I was heavy and I was into music so deeply. I just sat home a lot and practiced the piano and wrote and sang." Jerry Melton remembers her performance in a musical production of *The Merry Widow,* for which she had the lead role: "She was very talented, a truly charming young girl. Not too many people know it, but she also had a beautiful singing voice." Even today Diana Canova fans may not know it, for the actress's TV roles—in *Soap* and *Throb*—have not given her singing voice much exposure.

Though marijuana was in abundance on campus in those days, and peer pressure was surely considerable, Diana managed to keep fairly aloof from the drug scene, at least most of the time. "On the lawns of Hollywood High, I would be offered downers and such," she told *The Star* magazine. "I did some marijuana and some other things. I didn't do it for very long because deep down I knew it wasn't right."

Drugs were still proliferating at Hollywood High when *Dallas* costar Charlene Tilton attended the school in the mid-Seventies, but of far more concern was the issue of campus violence. "Have the restrooms locked during classes, but give all the teachers a key," was Charlene's reply to a newspaper poll in which students were asked for suggestions on how best to end campus violence. "That way, in case of emergency, the teacher would know who was in the bathroom."

The poll was conducted in 1974, Charlene's sophomore year, by which time she was already one of Hollywood High's most popular coeds. Her high school career would be long on activities, but short on scholastic achievement. Drama classes, cheerleading, and a variety of other extracurricular activities—including a stint at newswriting—kept her too busy to spend much time on homework. Besides, since she knew she wanted to be an actress, she saw little use for algebra, geography, and history. One of her worst subjects was French—she received a D her first year in the course, and failed the second.

Acting may have been Charlene's primary interest at school, and she participated in several productions, but according to Jerry Melton, she was not one of his most promising students. "She was a sweet girl," he says, "but she was overshadowed by girls like Elyssa Davalos, who was one of the biggest talents I ever had at school and ended up with most of the leads." Charlene performed in a 1975 one-act student production of *Pepys and Company* (based on the diaries of Samuel Pepys), and later in the spring play *Major Barbara* and the 1976 production of *Elizabeth I*, but all her roles were minor ones. Nevertheless, she was spotted by an agent during her senior year and offered a role in a Disney movie, *Freaky Friday*. A series of small TV parts soon followed.

As for her brief stint as a feature writer for the school

newspaper, only one bylined example survives, but it is enough to reveal that fifteen-year-old Charlene Tilton may have possessed a talent for writing. Her one credited contribution to the paper was an investigation behind a resurgence of student interest in surfing. Entitled "Surfers Mania Hits Once Again," the article is a standout, cleverly written, if a bit relentless in its deployment of watery metaphors. "Most fads come and go with the tides," it reads, "but the surfer craze floated ashore many years ago and is anchored here for many years to come."

Charlene Tilton was not the only celebrity to emerge from Hollywood High in 1976. Noted operatic soprano Aprile Millo also graduated that year. Fellow students remember young Aprile's superb performance in the title role of Hollywood High's production of *Hello, Dolly*. Jerry Melton remembers it too: "Needless to say, she had an incredible voice."

Hollywood High has enough problems as it is; we don't need to have disgusting movies about us circulating around the country. Do you really want the rest of the country thinking that Hollywood High girls love to have sex with midget mechanics at gas stations!!!???

> —From the school paper's editorial
> on the 1977 teen exploitation
> film, *Hollywood High*

*I*n its heyday, Hollywood High had always maintained high academic standards, with achievement levels comparable to those of the area's best private schools. It was long regarded by the mostly affluent families who populated the school district as a perfectly satisfactory college preparatory school. In order to graduate, students of Hollywood High were required to complete a well-rounded curriculum, which included as a mainstay the ability to write a flawless English composition; one error in spelling or punctuation could result in failure.

Predictably, the district's ethnic shift had a profound effect on the school's ability to maintain any semblance of its past record. In the Seventies waves of immigrant students from Southeast Asia and Central America were beginning to outnumber the American-born members of the student body. Writing essays in flawless English was an impossible goal once a hefty percentage of the students did not even speak the language. By 1977 Hollywood High was ranked in the distressingly low eighteenth percentile among California schools.

In an effort to cope with the problem, the district established a program called English as a Second Language, or ESL. Students with language difficulties were required to take the ESL classes before moving on to a regular course schedule. This was a step in the right direction, but obviously it would take years for the effects to be felt.

Meanwhile, the atmosphere on campus was not especially conducive to learning. Vandalism, violence, and theft were commonplace. Discipline was under heavy siege. Assemblies had become raucous, students were wandering on and off campus without the required permits, girls were wearing revealing outfits to school, and boys were walking around shirtless. School spirit had virtually disappeared—a 1979 pep rally attracted no more than twenty students. The school paper, renamed *The Sheik Press* in 1978, asked the student body whether it was still possible to "Achieve the Honorable."

Ironically, it was the 1977 release of a teen exploitation film called *Hollywood High* that managed to inspire a brief surge in school pride. Students were angry that the filmmakers had so blatantly capitalized on Hollywood High's sacred name and reputation, only to besmirch them with little regard for accuracy. According to the editors of *The Sheik Press*, the film had little to do with the school and was, in fact, filmed entirely off campus, except for two drive-by shots. The movie "portrays our teachers as feeble-minded perverted sickies," the paper raged, "and describes our students as sex-crazed morons whose main purpose in life seems to be getting stoned and having sexual relations in vans, or having spaghetti fights in pizzerias."

In the midst of all this, Hollywood High was looking forward to celebrating its Diamond Jubilee. The school would be seventy-five years old in November 1978, and a gala program commemorating the event was to be held in the auditorium. Students, alumni, and "an impressive array of dignitaries, including the mayor of Los Angeles, Tom Bradley," were expected to attend. Besieged as the school was with the problems of the moment, the Diamond Jubilee would be Hollywood High's chance to relive something of its past glory.

Sadly, the event turned out to be a bit of a disappointment. Mayor Bradley's limousine got stuck in an afternoon traffic snarl, preventing his arrival. Nor was he the only no-show. In fact, of all the dignitaries invited, only the local consul general of Brazil managed to make an appearance.

As usual, however, the Hollywood High theatrical production was outstanding—the only beacon in a sadly lackluster seventy-fifth anniversary. *Mame*, the musical comedy the drama department had chosen to produce as its contribution to the festivities, was directed by Jerry Melton. The title role was played by a youngster named Sharon Brown, whose acting credits at the time included over thirty commercials and stints with the national touring companies of *The Wiz* and *Maggie Flynn*. Her performance in Hollywood High's *Mame* was the high point of the Jubilee Celebration. Fittingly, Sharon Brown, class of 1979, is generally regarded as the last Hollywood High graduate to make a significant splash in show business. Her recent credits include lead roles in the Los Angeles production of *Dreamgirls* and the film version of *A Chorus Line*.

4.

Prostitutes who ply their trade on Sunset Boulevard during school hours have become a common sight to Hollywood High students, among whom some have supposedly become customers.

—From an article in
The Sheik Press, 1981

The early Eighties were perhaps the nadir of Hollywood High's long history. By the turn of the decade, fifty percent of the sophomore class failed a departmental English test given at the beginning of the semester. The school's finance office was burglarized, jewelry theft was rampant, false fire alarms were being set with distressing regularity, and, with all too heavy-handed an irony, the senior class chose a band called Organized Crime to play at the senior prom that year. In May 1983, the administration building was the victim of an arson attempt resulting in fifteen hundred dollars' worth of damages, and a teacher was severely beaten by three nonstudents in front of his class. Derelicts were regularly caught sleeping under the athletics field bleachers, and nonstudents were making the campus a second home. When asked by *The Sheik Press* if he would send a son or daughter to Hollywood High, Harry Major replied: "I would like to think that my child deserves something better. Hollywood High works on what I've called a 'schlepp und stagger' system, if you understand my basket German. It's a drag, and stagger around.

There is no cohesion, no sense of academic destiny or excellence."

Meanwhile, the surrounding area had deteriorated to such an extent that prostitutes plying their trade across the street from the school were clearly visible from the campus throughout much of the school day. Rumor had it that some of the students were regular customers, but according to an article in *The Sheik Press*, the prostitutes were anything but enthusiastic about the proximity of the campus. "According to prostitutes, the question is not whether the prostitution will affect the students," read the article, "but instead it is whether the students will affect the prostitution business. As one prostitute commented, 'During lunch time, kids are all over the place and men are embarrassed to come.'" The newspaper concluded with a wry observation: "Sunset Boulevard prostitution has made Hollywood High a unique educational institution. Where else can an English class diagram sentences inside a class, while looking outside the window to see how long it takes a prostitute to turn a trick?" A number of protests were lodged with the city, and the prostitutes were "persuaded" to relocate.

Though 1978's Diamond Jubilee program had been something of a disappointment, the school got another chance to relive its glorious past in November 1982, when students and alumni celebrated the Hollywood High Homecoming Hop, a special event organized by alumna Stefanie Powers to promote a special high school episode of her series, *Hart to Hart*. Powers, who had graduated from Hollywood High in 1960, chose 1960 nostalgia as the hop's theme; students, alumni, and a coterie of stars, dressed in saddle shoes, letter sweaters, and pleated skirts, all gathered in the school's gymnasium, twisting the night away. With Powers (who wore a "Kennedy for President" button over her letter sweater) was her *Hart to Hart* costar Robert Wagner, who was overheard admitting that he used to cruise Hollywood High to catch a glimpse of all the pretty girls on campus. Powers's classmate Linda Evans also attended the event, as did alumnus Alan Hale, Jr., producer Allan Carr, and the class of 1951's star pupil, Carol Burnett. After the ROTC troop and the cheerleaders had marched through the gym, followed by the drill team and the pom-pom girls, Burnett grabbed the microphone and blew a resounding Bronx cheer to the boy on whom she had had an unrequited crush all through high school.

5.

The community of Hollywood, once a glamorous haven for movie stars and tourists, slowly began to decline in the early Seventies. Yet within the last few years, a serious campaign to revitalize the community began and slowly Hollywood is cleaning up its act.

—From *The Sheik Press*, 1982

In September 1983 Hollywood High got a new principal. Willard B. Hansen was no stranger to the campus—he had taught English at the school from 1954 to 1962, before leaving to become principal of nearby Reseda High School. A Harvard graduate with thirty years of teaching experience, Hansen is an affable man with a sharp sense of humor and an easygoing disposition.

Hansen's mandate was clear—Hollywood High's academic standing and educational atmosphere were in drastic need of improvement—and he wasted no time in getting the process under way. His first significant action as principal, and a highly controversial one, was to erect a fence around part of the campus. "I was appalled at the lack of security when I came here," he told a local newspaper reporter in 1984. "Derelicts regularly sleep on campus. We've had a nonstudent walk into a music classroom and play the piano, rather well, I'm told. Teachers over the years have had to deal with a continuous stream of people with no business on campus. What bothered me was that no one seemed to care." In spite

of protests from some alumni and local restaurant owners who claimed the fence would destroy their busi-
nesses, the move was endorsed by parents and local
police. Since 1983, according to Hansen, there has been
only one assault on a teacher.

With the campus secured from outside marauders, a
host of other problems still remain, some of them nearly
intractable. To combat the presence of drugs on campus,
an antidrug education program called DARE (Drug
Abuse Resistance Education) was instituted in 1983. Two
Los Angeles police officers conducted the course, and it
appears to have had some success. "Project DARE is not
only steering students away from drugs," observed the
school paper in 1985, "it appears to be having a positive
side effect of helping to improve academic performance." Though there are no precise statistics on the annual number of dropouts, Willard Hansen has described
the problem as "severe." Absenteeism also plagues the
school, with fifteen percent of the students registering as
absent per day.

In an effort to change with the times, a number of
Hollywood High's old traditions have been discarded.
Though students still need permits to leave the campus,
there are no more detention study halls for those who
disobey the rules. "Discipline is up to the individual
teachers," Hansen says, "and the parents have been very
cooperative." Mandatory assemblies, once a mainstay of
student life, have been dropped as well. "They take time
away from the instructional program," Hansen claims,
"and two thousand students in an auditorium can easily
get out of hand."

Test scores have been going up within the last few

years, not radically, but bit by bit. Though Hollywood High remains in a low percentile academically, the outlook is encouraging. The class of 1986 saw sixty percent of its members going on to some form of higher education. Hansen also detects a slight improvement in school spirit, with more students joining clubs and attending pep rallies. "We've made some progress," he says, "but we still have a long way to go."

Student dramatics have also undergone a profound change. In 1981 the Los Angeles school board established the Performing Arts Magnet School, a special program designed primarily to achieve ethnic integration among all students interested in studying drama. Not surprisingly, given its past, Hollywood High was chosen as one of several homes for the new program. Magnet School students, who are bussed in from all over the L.A. district, take regular classes at Hollywood High, in addition to attending special drama courses and participating in Magnet theatrical productions. Today all Hollywood High productions are Magnet productions.

Unfortunately, the program got off to a rocky start. The first year—1981—eighty students were enrolled, and according to Jerry Melton, the results were far from satisfactory: "We had some bad-news Charlies in that first group," he says. "They'd just get off the bus and disappear into the streets of Hollywood." Absenteeism at rehearsals was so rampant that Melton was forced to cancel 1982's production of *The Music Man,* the first time in its history a Hollywood High production was ever canceled.

Since then, the Magnet School program has improved considerably. Today, with an enrollment of 225, the Hollywood High Magnet students stage a total of five major productions a year, as well as four minor ones. Melton claims that discipline is excellent and that his attrition rate is low, with an average of only ten percent of his students dropping out before completion of the term. (Hollywood High's overall dropout rate is significantly higher.) Magnet productions have won numerous local awards—a particularly impressive feat since Magnet students are chosen not by audition, but by computer, in order to insure a proper racial mix. Additional good news is that tension between the regular Hollywood High students and the Magnet pupils (or "Maggots," as they've been nicknamed) is minimal.

And there are other encouraging signs as well. One would expect a place like Hollywood High to be a hotbed of racial tension, but according to Hansen, this has never been a major problem at the school. In fact, the student body, which is now comprised of representatives from over seventy-five different countries, has made a special effort to celebrate its racial mix. The 1986 *Poinsettia,* for example, was subtitled *Hollywood High International,* and its cover featured a globe embossed on a field of black. Black was specifically chosen because, as the editors pointed out, "it is the mixture of all colors." Wrote one senior in 1986's end-of-the-year issue of *The Sheik Press*: "Hollywood High School takes great pride in its cultural diversity. Every day, both students and faculty learn about many different cultures and lifestyles that go far beyond the daily curriculum."

6.

I Jesuric Federico, predict that there's a bright tomorrow if you work harder.

I Vrej Sarkissian, do predict that with my training at Hollywood High School, I will be successful in life.

I Regina Orellana, predict that in the future no one is going to throw my friends and I out of restaurants for being noisy.

—A sample of senior class
predictions, June 1986

*O*n a bright, sunny afternoon in January 1987, the kind of day that must have inspired the pioneer filmmakers to settle in this neck of the woods some seventy-seven years ago, Hollywood High's alumni are gathered just outside the school's auditorium to celebrate Alumni Day. It is either the seventy-ninth or eightieth such event. No one is quite sure anymore, there have been so many. There are no famous faces in the crowd, just ordinary old-timers and a smattering of younger alumni for whom school spirit did not suddenly evaporate on graduation day. Dress is casual, but most of the older men are wearing jackets and ties, and the women appear to have spent the previous day at the hairdresser's. After all, this is Hollywood High, and Hollywood High is special.

After registering at a flimsy desk manned by two spirited graduates of the class of 1926, the alumni drift into the inevitable clusters and begin to travel in that familiar territory known as "the Good Old Days." Some pore over old yearbooks, while the class clowns and school orators of yesteryear easily revert to their old styles. Though many of these people have not seen a classroom in fifty years, it is not difficult to distinguish the wallflowers from the cutups.

Suddenly a lunch bell clangs and a raucous gaggle of students—clad in T-shirts, blue jeans, torn sweatshirts—passes through the crowd of alumni on the way to the cafeteria. A few of the old-timers cannot help but shake their heads with dismay over what destiny has dealt their fair alma mater.

"In my day," remarks a member of the class of 1934, "if you'd come to school dressed like that, Mr. Foley would've sent you right home, no questions asked. . . ."

"Trouble is, there's no discipline today," observes another, a World War II veteran. "Why, even the teachers dress like the students. Our teachers wore suits and ties to school. We looked up to them, respected them, and they taught us more than just English or math—they taught us values and standards. . . ."

"You know, I wanted to come to one of the productions," says a graduate of the class of 1938, a former high school thespian, "but I'm afraid to walk the streets of this neighborhood at night. You should've seen Hollywood Boulevard when I was a senior here. Such a difference."

Later, the party moves into the auditorium for the second installment of the celebration. When everyone is seated, the Hollywood High School band blasts forth with a rousing Sousa march, which, in keeping with age-old tradition, is noticeably out of tune. With school spirit rising to a fever pitch, the 1987 senior class, which has been invited to the festivities, files noisily into the room. After a few addresses and the presentation of a plaque to a local fast-food merchant, the lights dim and a slide show on the history of Hollywood commences. Inevitably, the first few slides are projected upside down, and a number of the seniors cannot resist the overwhelming temptation to shout out the usual choice remarks. The alumni are unperturbed by the display. Some things never change.

As legend has it, this auditorium is haunted by a deceased Hollywood High custodian, known around campus as Olivia. As the story goes, Olivia was so enamored of the school's drama students, she vowed to return after her death to be close to them. "Ghost Olivia," as she is called, has resided here since 1960, and periodic "proof" of her existence has kept the legend alive over the years. Once she allegedly tried to speak to a janitor; on another occasion, a spotlight mysteriously switched on by itself; and in the fall of 1974, a column of bluish-white light was seen in the balcony staircase by two students. When the two curious boys approached the beam, they were enveloped by an eerie chill.

But Ghost Olivia is not alone, for a profusion of apparitions haunts this venerable old campus. The spectres are everywhere. All you need is the imagination to see them. Close your eyes and you'll envision a freckle-faced redhead named Alexis Smith tap-dancing on the stage; and what about that tall, lanky youth carrying that spear a little too self-consciously—isn't that Joel McCrea? Glance out at the athletics field and you'll spot young Jason Robards dashing around the track, and there's little Ricky Nelson going out for a pass. And who's that brash youngster pulling up right on the front lawn with his new Ford convertible? Why, it's Mickey Rooney!

Just to the left of us, in the center of what is now a faculty parking lot, Fay Wray would eat her lunch on the lawn, shaded by wild pepper trees, and it was in the atrium of the old administration building, its foundation compromised by an earthquake in 1933, that young Bill Shockley, clad in a toga, marched with the other slaves in 1927's annual Roman banquet. A few feet away are the paved-over remains of the tree that Stefanie Powers chopped down as a prank. And the famous Top Hat Cafe, once located just across the street, is now a Texaco station.

If nothing else, the history of Hollywood High is a vivid study in contrasts. Yesterday it was the cradle of the stars, an academic haven set in the midst of elegant boulevards and chichi nightclubs; today it is a miniature melting pot, struggling valiantly to achieve the honorable in the face of urban blight. Few of the old traditions have survived, and one cannot help but wonder what James O. Churchill would say if he could see his school today. No doubt he would hold forth with one of the axioms for which he was so esteemed.

Perhaps one day Hollywood High will produce another Jason Robards or another Lana Turner. After all, even at the worst of times, the quality of its theatrical presentations never waned. Two world wars and one Great Depression failed to stifle the caliber of its stage plays and musicals, and even when campus violence was at its worst, the drama group managed to nab every trophy in the district. Lately, the phones have been ringing again with theatrical agents calling in search of new clients, and it is the rare production that does not have at least two or three talent scouts in the audience, hoping to make a discovery. Drama director Jerry Melton, for one, is optimistic. When asked about the school's future, his retort is generally the same: "Who knows which of these kids may someday make it big?"

NOTES

PART ONE

(p.xi)   "Hollywood High. Bigger'n life." Carol Burnett, *One More Time* (New York, Random House, Inc., 1986), p. 134.

(p.xi)   "We rattled our way" Lana Turner, *Lana: The Lady, the Legend, the Truth* (New York: E.P. Dutton, Inc., 1982).

(p.9)   "A ridiculous piece of extravagance" Local farmer.

(p.13)   "Six months rent free" Mr. H.J. Whitley (Hollywood real estate tycoon), local paper.

(p.15)   "The students selected their course" James Otis Churchill (principal), *First Annual Report of the Hollywood Union High School*, 1 July 1904.

(p.16)   "As physical culture is part" James Otis Churchill, *First Annual Report of the Hollywood Union High School*.

(p.17)   "The atmosphere of the school" From a 1909 pamphlet on Hollywood High.

(p.17)   "The costliest, most thoroughly equipped" *The Hollywood Sentinel*.

(p.20)   "one of the most thrilling" *The Hollywood Sentinel*, November 1904.

(p.20)   "The very first day" Student, *The Poinsettia*, 1906.

(p.26)   "our pleasant task" Student, "Foreword," *The Poinsettia*, 1909.

(p.33)   "The citizens spent long afternoons" Agnes De Mille, 1913.

(p.35)   "Most Hollywoodians went about their tasks" Evelyn F. Scott, *Hollywood: When Silents Were Golden* (New York: McGraw-Hill, Inc., 1972).

(p.40)   "I used to sneak" Ruth Roland, *The Hollywood High School News*, 3 January 1930.

(p.42)   "LOOK OUT KAISER BILL!" Editor, *The Hollywood High School News*, 1917.

(p.44)   "Old Caesar was a gay old chap" Student, *The Poinsettia*, 1917.

(p.48)   "The War is over" Invitation to the Alumni Banquet, 1919.

(p.52)   "When I said" Mack Sennett.

(p.53)   "transformed from one of the" "Hollywood Hi-Stars," *The Los Angeles Times*, 16 December 1928.

PART TWO

(p.57)   "Sophomore: Have you ever taken chloroform?" Student, *The Poinsettia*, 1920.

(p.58)   "At Hollywood is a colony" Member of U.S. Congress, *Congressional Record*, 1922.

(p.58)   "Many of the current magazines" Student, *The Hollywood High School News*, December 1921.

(p.59)   "We read all about the so-called scandals" Alumnus, Interview with Author.

(p.65)   "The Hand in Human Progress" Title of the winning submission for Hollywood High's biology essay contest, *The Hollywood High School News*, November 1923.

(p.72)   "I didn't realize then" Fay Wray, Interview with Author.

(p.72)   "I loved school" Fay Wray, Interview with Author.

(p.73)   "After school, I would go right home" Fay Wray, Interview with Author.

(p.73)   "He was an inspiration" Fay Wray, Interview with Author.

(p.73)   "I played a kind of vestal virgin" Fay Wray, Interview with Author.

(p.73)   "they didn't discover me" Fay Wray, Interview with Author.

(p.75)   "Keep out of this film acting business" Ruth Roland, quoted in *The Hollywood High School News*, 3 January 1930.

(p.76)   "He was a tall youth" Evelyn F. Scott, *Hollywood: When Silents Were Golden* (New York: McGraw-Hill, Inc., 1972).

(p.76)   "I was the only one" Joel McCrea, Interview with Author.

(p.76)   "He was a nice kid" Classmate of Joel McCrea, Interview with Author.

(p.76)   "I was kind of a flop in school" Joel McCrea, Interview with Author.

(p.77)   "I had a walk-on part" Joel McCrea, Interview with Author.

(p.77)   "Come on, kid" Otis Clasky, quoted by Joel McCrea in his Interview with the Author.

(p.85)   "If your family didn't own a radio" Alumnus, Interview with Author.

(p.85)   "The motion picture theatre owners" *Photoplay*, 1925.

(p.88)   "Any undue familiarity" Blanche Graham and Gertrude Graham, "Good Manners," pamphlet (Los Angeles: Hollywood High, 1927).

(p.89)   "Loud talking, slang, boisterous manners" "Good Manners."

(p.90)   "A girl may ask a boy" "Good Manners."

(p.91)   "A gentleman" "Good Manners."

(p.92)   "High school students have not reached" Editor, *The Hollywood High School News*, April 1927.

(p.94)   "Frantic parents, some said to be prominent and wealthy" *The Los Angeles Herald*, October 1929.

(p.95)   "Mary Pickford was accompanied" Student, *The Hollywood High School News*, April 1929.

(p.97)   "He was warm, positive, and very visible" Glenn McConnell, Interview with Author.

PART THREE

(p.103) "WALL ST. LAYS AN EGG" *Variety*, October 1929.

(p.105) "Movie theatres are the last" Carl Laemmle, 1929.

(p.108) "Can you fall gracefully?" Student, *The Hollywood High School News*, February 1932.

(p.111) "Things were tight" Bill Lindsay, Interview with Author.

(p.111) "My parents never let on" Alexis Smith, Interview with Author.

(p.115) "In his oration" Student, *The Poinsettia*, 1930.

(p.120) "There were a few" Alumnus, Interview with Author.

(p.121) "We were still" Bill Lindsay, Interview with Author.

(p.123) "You wouldn't kidney would you?" Student, *The Hollywood High School News*, February 1936.

(p.126) "Would you like to know" Mickey Rooney, *I.E.: An Autobiography* (New York: Putnam Publishing Group, Inc., 1965).

(p.127) "The first thing he did" "Hollywood's Fabulous Brat,"
The Saturday Evening Post, 6 December 1947.

(p.127) "The first time I saw her" Mickey Rooney, *I.E.: An Auto-biography.*

(p.128) "She was the most incredibly" Nanette Fabray, "Famous
Gals of Hollywood High," *Hollywood Studio Magazine,*
October-November 1974.

(p.128) "It was quite incredible" Alexis Smith, Interview with
Author.

(p.128) "We did not go to Hollywood" Lana Turner, "My Private Life," *Woman's Home Companion,* December
1951.

(p.129) "One of the horrors" Lana Turner, *Lana: The Lady, the
Legend, the Truth* (New York: E.P. Dutton, Inc., 1982).

(p.129) "Somebody once compared" Lana Turner, *Lana: The
Lady, the Legend, the Truth.*

(p.129) "She started the course late" Cyrille Block, Interview
with Author.

(p.129) "She was totally unaffected" Lois Barthelmess, Interview
with Author.

(p.130) "The malt shop was a social club" Mickey Rooney, *I.E.:
An Autobiography.*

(p.130) "What was it like" Mickey Rooney, *I.E.: An Autobiography.*

(p.130) "Once we all went to a show" Lois Barthelmess, Interview with Author.

(p.131) "She was a tiny little girl" Alumna, Interview with Author.

(p.133) "Alexis Smith gave an excellent account" Student, *The
Poinsettia,* 1938.

(p.135) "She was a popular girl" Bill Lindsay, Interview with
Author.

(p.136) "I was very impressed" Alexis Smith, Interview with Author.

(p.136) "Miss Heep was a big influence" Alexis Smith, Interview
with Author.

(p.138) "I was socially inept" Alexis Smith, Interview with Author.

(p.138) "I took typing" Alexis Smith, Interview with Author.

(p.139) "Every time I get out of my berth" Alexis Smith, Interview with Author.

(p.139)   "When we returned" Alexis Smith, Interview with Author.

(p.141)   "Lovely, happy girl" Cyrille Block, Interview with Author.

(p.141)   "a level-headed, down to earth" Bill Lindsay, Interview with Author.

(p.141)   "I went through life" Nanette Fabray, *The Los Angeles Herald-Examiner,* 24 April 1983.

(p.143)   "Temporary hard water" Science teacher, series on test "boners," *The Hollywood High School News,* September 1935.

PART FOUR

(p.151)   "There is one thing" Louis Foley (principal), assembly speech: quoted in *The Hollywood High School News,* 3 December 1941.

(p.154)   "In the feature race" Student, *The Hollywood High School News,* May 1939.

(p.154)   "spent a lot of time" Jason Robards, Jr., "One Rail," *The New Yorker,* 3 January 1959.

(p.159)   "Teacher: What was the age of Pericles?" Student, quoted in *The Hollywood High School News,* April 1942.

(p.161)   "Their marksmanship was rotten" *Los Angeles Times,* 24 February 1942.

(p.163)   "Everybody thought it would be over" Glenn Mc-Connell, Interview with Author.

(p.165)   "I only ask that when I die" Student, *The Hollywood High School News,* June 1942.

(p.167)   "As for romance—" *Look* (article on Hollywood High), 1941.

(p.167)   "the girls are perhaps more style-conscious" *Look* (article on Hollywood High), 1941.

(p.170)   "In those days" Warren Christopher, Interview with Author.

(p.172)   "I always had a job" Warren Christopher, Interview with Author.

(p.172)   "I organized a type of radio news" Warren Christopher, Interview with Author.

(p.174)   "The Japanese-American students" Adalene Maki, Interview with Author.

NOTES

(p.174) "It was a very sad time" Warren Christopher, Interview with Author.

(p.176) "BUY STAMPS TO BLACK OUT DER FUEHRER!" Slogan for Hollywood High defense stamp drive, *The Hollywood High School News,* October 1942.

(p.178) "School dances were dreadful" Adalene Maki, Interview with Author.

(p.181) "I wanted to play football" James Garner, Interview, *Playboy,* March 1977.

(p.183) "Dick made no effort" *The Hollywood Citizen News,* 12 March 1945.

(p.183) "I saw these good-looking girls" James Garner, Interview, *Playboy,* March 1977.

(p.185) "My buddies used to bet me" James Garner, Interview, *Playboy,* March 1977.

(p.186) "He admits he was a juvenile" Hedda Hopper, *Chicago Tribune,* 19 October 1958.

(p.188) "It's a great life" Louis Foley: quoted in *The Hollywood High School News,* January 1944.

(p.193) "I didn't catch on" Marcel Ophuls, *Current Biography,* June 1977.

(p.194) "Bobby sox lose the shape" Miss Hollywood, *The Hollywood High School News,* 19 March 1945.

(p.195) "If you didn't show up" Rosita Smith, Interview with Author.

PART FIVE

(p.199) "People will soon get tired" A studio executive on the future of television.

(p.204) "I remember one girl" Alumnus, Interview with Author.

(p.204) "We'd see a happy" Carol Burnett, *One More Time* (New York: Random House, Inc., 1986).

(p.206) "Sometimes a guy or two" Carol Burnett, *One More Time.*

(p.207) "I felt lost" Carol Burnett, *One More Time.*

(p.208) "That year, the Hollywood High" Carol Burnett, *One More Time.*

(p.211) "Etikut: It's sorta considered" Carol Burnett, "Rovin I," *The Hollywood High School News,* 1951.

(p.213) "Three ways to avoid" Student, *The Hollywood High School News,* February 1953.

(p.214)   "They'll wear toilet seats" Paramount executive.

(p.214)   "A nine-day wonder" Alfred Hitchcock.

(p.214)   "We were always up for" Alumnus, Interview with Author.

(p.218)   "It took me until" Sally Kellerman, *Playgirl*, November 1975.

(p.219)   "Sure, there was still this aura" John Ingle (drama director), Interview with Author.

(p.220)   "One afternoon I decided" Ozzie Nelson, *Ozzie,* (New Jersey: Prentice-Hall, Inc., 1973).

(p.223)   "My first month at Hollywood High" Sally Kellerman, *Playgirl*, November 1975.

(p.224)   "a really good time" Mike Farrell, Interview with Author.

(p.226)   "I was never a troublemaker" Mike Farrell, Interview with Author.

(p.226)   "I was a lazy student" Mike Farrell, Interview with Author.

(p.226)   "Cool was chasing girls" Mike Farrell, Interview with Author.

(p.227)   "I spent most of my high school" Mike Farrell, Interview with Author.

(p.231)   "He was an average student" One of Rick Nelson's English teachers, Interview with Author.

(p.231)   "He was not revered" Mike Farrell, Interview with Author.

(p.233)   "Friday night slumber" Student, *The Hollywood High School News*, April, 1957.

PART SIX

(p.239)   "We're not nasty" New football cheer, *The Hollywood High School News*, January 1961.

(p.245)   "I grew up" Stefanie Powers.

(p.245)   "There was no play time" John Ingle, Interview with Author.

(p.248)   "It was a fairly big tree" Willard B. Hansen (principal), Interview with Author.

(p.248)   "There we were" Stefanie Powers, *People*, 22 November 1982.

(p.251) "I must have been" Linda Evans, "Roughing It with Linda Evans," *The Ladies' Home Journal*, November 1986.

(p.251) "I was shocked" Linda Evans, Interview with Sue Russell.

(p.252) "Nobody paid any attention" Tuesday Weld, *The Los Angeles Herald-Examiner*, 15 October 1972.

(p.253) "I was working in the office" Willard B. Hansen, Interview with Author.

(p.253) "I hated it" Yvette Mimieux, studio biography.

(p.254) "talented youngster" John Ingle, Interview with Author.

(p.254) "She was certainly not" Willard B. Hansen, Interview with Author.

(p.256) "Sex is not the only subject" Editor, *The News*, March 1964.

(p.261) "She was a dynamite talent" John Ingle, Interview with Author.

(p.262) "I was never" Meredith Baxter Birney, "On the Set with Family Ties," *The Ladies' Home Journal*, May 1986.

(p.262) "Whenever anyone asked me" Barbara Hershey, Interview with Author.

(p.262) "I was a responsible student" Barbara Hershey, Interview with Author.

(p.264) "very shy and very naive" Barbara Hershey, Interview with Author.

(p.264) "Drama removed me" Barbara Hershey, Interview with Author.

(p.264) "He was a great drama teacher" Barbara Hershey, Interview with Author.

(p.265) "I adored her" John Ingle, Interview with Author.

(p.265) "I chose the nuttiest parts" Barbara Hershey, Interview with Author.

(p.265) "I didn't really learn" Barbara Hershey, Interview with Author.

(p.266) "I didn't give a damn" John Clifford, *The Los Angeles Times*, 19 August 1969.

(p.267) "It was one" John Ritter, Interview with Author.

(p.267) "I had a pretty big" John Ritter, Interview with Author.

(p.267) "I had two goals" John Ritter, Interview with Author.

(p.267) "He was the type" John Swinford (English Department Chair): quoted in *The Sheik Press*, June 1982.

PART SEVEN

NOTES

(p.290)   "On the lawns of Hollywood High" Diana Canova, *The Star,* 7 April 1981.

(p.291)   "She was a sweet girl" Jerry Melton, Interview with Author.

(p.292)   "Needless to say" Jerry Melton, Interview with Author.

(p.293)   "Hollywood High has enough problems" *The News,* 7 October 1977.

(p.296)   "Prostitutes who ply their trade" *The Sheik Press,* 30 October 1981.

(p.299)   "The community of Hollywood" *The Sheik Press,* 9 June 1982.

(p.299)   "I was appalled" Willard B. Hansen, *The Los Angeles Times,* 26 January 1984.

(p.300)   "Discipline is up to" Willard B. Hansen, Interview with Author.

(p.301)   "We've made some progress" Willard B. Hansen, Interview with Author.

(p.301)   "We had some bad-news Charlies" Jerry Melton, Interview with Author.

(p.303)   "I Jesuric Federico" "Class Predictions," *The Sheik Press,* June 1986.

(p.304)   "In my day" Alumnus, Interview with Author.

(p.304)   "Trouble is, there's no discipline" Alumnus, Interview with Author.

(p.304)   "You know, I wanted to" Alumnus, Interview with Author.

(p.307)   "Who knows which of these kids" Jerry Melton, Interview with Author.

INDEX

INDEX

ABOUT THE AUTHOR

JOHN BLUMENTHAL is a Los Angeles–based writer whose articles, interviews, and essays have appeared in *Playboy, Esquire,* and *Punch.* He is the author of *The Official Hollywood Handbook, The Case of the Hardboiled Dicks, The Tinseltown Murders,* and coauthor of *Love's Reckless Rash.*